RAVE REVIEWS FOR PowerSpeak

"I heartily recommend this book to business professionals who want to enhance their ability to communicate with energy and proficiency ... Dorothy's book is head and shoulders above the rest!"
—C. David Brown, Past President,
    National Association for Corporate Speaker Activities

"This work will be of tremendous value to countless executives ... A valuable contribution to the art of public speaking."
—John J. McManus, Executive Vice President,
    Professional Insurance
    Mass-Marketing Association (PIMA)

"Invaluable ... For those who are serious about improving their presentations (and all of us should be), everything is here: not only what to avoid but how to do it right."
—George Gross, Executive Director,
    New York State Financial Control Board

"Packed with invaluable advice for everyone ... What a terrific book!"
—Michael LeBoeuf, author of
    GMP: The Greatest Management Principle in the World

ABOUT THE AUTHOR

DOROTHY LEEDS has been applauded by more than 100,000 people, having keynoted at hundreds of conferences and conventions, including regular appearances at the National Speakers Association. She is president of Organization Technologies Inc., a management and sales consulting firm. Ms. Leeds has organized and conducted communication seminars and training programs for major corporations here and abroad, set up Speaker's Bureaus, and trained thousands of executives and salespeople.

Most Berkley Books are available at special quantity discounts for bulk pur-
chases for sales promotions, premiums, fund raising, or educational use.
Special books or book excerpts can also be created to fit specific needs.

For details, write or telephone Special Markets, The Berkley Publishing
Group, 200 Madison Avenue, New York, New York 10016; (212) 951-8800.

POWERSPEAK

DOROTHY LEEDS

BERKLEY BOOKS, NEW YORK

To Three Very Special Mothers:
Toni Adelsberg, Anna P. Robertson, and
Elly Adelsberg
With Love

Acknowledgments

Special thanks and deep appreciation to:

Nina Frost, for her enormous patience, talent, and professionalism. This book would not have been possible without her.

PJ Dempsey, my very special editor and friend, who makes even the most tedious task a pleasure.

Jeanne Kramer and her capable staff, for making PowerSpeak a public event.

Maureen A. Clark, a meticulous and creative copy editor.

Eve Collyer, the greatest speech teacher of them all.

Sharyn Kolberg, for her constructive and encouraging editorial help.

Carol Leigh Gribble, without whose good cheer and administrative help I wouldn't have had the time.

Debra Sherline, a dear friend and a great publicist who makes so much happen.

Nido Qubein, a mentor and inspiration who started me on my literary career.

Dan Kennedy and Joel Beck, the dynamic duo who help so much in so many ways.

The National Speakers Association and all its loving and sharing members.

Mike Wickett, a warm, supportive fan who was one of the first to recognize the power of PowerSpeak.

Layne Sharton, for her encouragement and for making recording a pleasure.

Michael LeBoeuf, for his constant advice, warm friendship, and funny jokes.

Vera Derr, Toni Boyle, and the Nightingale-Conant staff, for their enthusiasm for PowerSpeak and my talents as a speaker.

Angie Howard, for her initial belief in my ability to teach public speaking.

The Duke Power Company, Michael Moody, and the Management Development Staff, for the ongoing opportunity to expand my teaching skills.

Joel Weldon, for his generosity.

Rich Di Georgio and Mobil Oil, for their support of the PowerSpeak system.

And to all the associations, corporations, and universities who graciously provide me a platform upon which to practice the PowerSpeak system.

Contents

Preface

Why another book on public speaking? I looked at the books available on this subject, and I found that not one book answered all my questions. As a teacher of public speaking I would have needed at least four different texts, so I decided to include it all in one book for myself, my students, and the companies and associations for whom I work. This is more than a book on public speaking: This is a book to help people who *communicate* learn how to make those *communications* more interesting, more lively, and more persuasive.

The title *PowerSpeak* refers to adding power to all your speaking—being persuasive whether you are serving customers, talking to subordinates, or hoping to talk your boss into a raise. Many of the chapters in this book (e.g. those on power language and body language) refer to topics that can be used in all types of everyday communication, not just platform speaking.

PowerSpeak is not only for people who make formal presentations. It is for teachers, for salespeople, and for anyone who conducts or participates in meetings. It is a book to make us all aware of the accessible and wonderful tools at our disposal. With persuasive speaking becoming so important and valued a skill, this book fills the need for a simple but complete text.

Through my years as an actress, an executive, and a speaker I searched for easy ways to get information across to others and to help others use the value of speaking as I used it to help myself. Through words and a strong delivery—although I am only 5′1″—I am able to command an audience.

If you don't have the attention of the other person or

persons, you are not communicating. No matter how good your idea, if it doesn't get through or doesn't get sold, you are not communicating. To be an effective speaker, you must be persuasive. You must be a salesperson with words and ideas. This is the basic concept strongly and uniquely addressed by the PowerSpeak system.

Introduction

What You Need to Know Before

You Read *PowerSpeak*

Make thyself a craftsman in speech, for thereby thou shalt gain the upper hand. —Inscription Found in a 3,000-year-old Egyptian Tomb

If you can't tell a book by its cover, at least the title should make clear what you are getting for your money. *Power-Speak* promises—and delivers—a lot.

I have designed it to be an all-encompassing aid for *anyone* who has to speak in public, whether that means a meeting with your boss, an important phone call, or a formal presentation to a hundred people. You can follow the chapters in order as in a course text, or you can study them one at a time as you need them. If you do all the projects, follow the self-evaluations, and practice the exercises included, I guarantee you will become a Power Speaker.

PowerSpeak addresses a problem that faces almost everyone in the business world today: how to increase your personal and professional ''power'' in order to make more sales, to move up to a better position, or to be more effective in your present position. The way you speak affects people's perceptions of you in meetings, during phone conversations, and in all your daily one-on-one relationships.

The ''power'' in the title comes from how people see you: Effective communicators are *perceived* as more powerful than their less verbal counterparts. Getting this power to work for you involves two steps: recognizing how crucial public speaking is and then improving your own abilities. This book is designed to sharpen those abilities in a way different from that of any other book on the market.

NOT JUST A BOOK—A COMPLETE COURSE

I have designed this book to answer all the questions that have come up through my years of teaching experience and to provide practical and professional techniques—to be a complete guide to public-speaking success. It is divided into four sections.

1. *Getting ready.* Why speaking adds to your power, how to banish fear, and how to prepare a presentation thoroughly.
2. *The six major speaking faults.* What they are and how to avoid them. This fault system works because people learn more quickly if they focus on what to *avoid*, rather than study a long list of the things they need to do right.
3. *The basics.* An in-depth look at the mechanics of openings, transitions, and conclusions.
4. *The fine points.* These chapters are filled with expert tips on handling humor, visual aids, the media, improving body language, and more.

Each chapter covers an area that, once mastered, adds to your power as a speaker. And to help you learn and put ideas to work immediately, each chapter includes tests that highlight the most important concepts and projects that allow you to practice those concepts. Where appropriate, I have also included handy checklists and questionnaires that will help you evaluate other speakers and track your own progress.

This interactive format makes *PowerSpeak* a veritable course in public speaking and presenting; if you take the time to take advantage of this format, you will learn not just by reading but by doing—*before* you have to give your next presentation.

Part I

Getting Ready to Be a

Powerful Speaker

1

How Public Speaking

Adds to Your Power

If all my talents and powers were to be taken from me by some unscrutable Providence, and I had my choice of keeping but one, I would unhesitatingly ask to be allowed to keep the Power of Speaking, for through it I would quickly recover all the rest. —Daniel Webster

What do the words *public speaking* bring to mind? Large halls and after-dinner ramblings? Executive seminars where you listen to a speaker expert in some key area of business? Politicians at election time? These answers are all correct, but big events and big names are just the tip of the public-speaking iceberg. Public speaking embraces not only the formal settings for speeches but also myriad events in any businessperson's day.

Public speaking affects every aspect of communication. It refers to your ability to get ideas across and to inform and persuade your audience. Even though most people admit to disliking it, everyone has to rely on his speaking abilities in meetings, on the phone, when asking for a raise, or when explaining procedures to a new employee. There are two varieties of business communication: written and spoken. And while many managers and executives complain about the number of memos they have to write, they communicate verbally much more often.

Yet many people persist in divorcing lectern-style public speaking from the speaking required in a one-on-one meeting with the boss. They think the former is a very formal event requiring preparation, and the latter can be done off-the-cuff. It can be, but the results won't distinguish you. Powerful people in business know how to put the power of speaking to work for them *whenever* they are communicating verbally. Those who don't think of themselves as public speakers within their companies probably aren't perceived as good speakers either, and they lose the aura that goes along with being known as an effective communicator. Or worse, they have a reputation for being dull, unsure of themselves, and weak.

The Not-So-Hidden Benefits of Powerful Speaking

I have seen what a newfound speaking ability can do for a person. Being a good presenter makes you *visible*, and in corporations, money, resources, and power flow to the visible high achiever. The visibility that speaking abilities give you becomes part of your overall professional growth. A colleague of mine at a large Fortune 500 company moved through the ranks with startling speed and ease. Many of his peers were just as competent, but he was a very good public speaker; his presentations were effective, persuasive events. He had an undeniable edge.

I also watched the careers of two executives at a large manufacturing firm. She was a highly persuasive speaker who had studied public speaking and ran dynamic meetings. She really knew how to inform *and* persuade. He, on the other hand, was a dull speaker. After five years, she was vice-president of their division, and he was still a manager. Needless to say, the executives may well have been equally competent. If you don't use public speaking to your advantage, someone else will use it to his.

There is just so much spotlight to go around, and it's a given that speakers occupy it regularly. Presenting in public is advertising with subtlety: You are displaying your abilities without touting them. As the old rhyme reminds us:

The codfish lays ten thousand eggs, the homely hen lays
   one.
The codfish never cackles to tell us what she's done;
and so we scorn the codfish while the homely hen we
   prize.
It only goes to show you that it pays to advertise.

The Six Major Speaking Faults

I have listened to *hundreds* of speeches. I have twelve
years of teaching experience and fifteen years of experience consulting with professionals. I have given hundreds
of workshops and trained more than ten thousand executives. The more I listened to people's presentations and
speeches, the more I recognized a "pattern" of flaws that
led to ineffective communication. And I discovered that in
all these hundreds of speeches there were *six major speaking faults* that occur over and over again, even among experienced speakers.

The more I teach public speaking, the more convinced
I become about the power of the six speaking faults. If
any one of them is present—even if you are doing everything else right—your talk loses most of its effectiveness.
Here are the six major speaking faults:

1. *An unclear purpose.* You want to motivate your audience in a certain way, but they would never know it
   from your meandering presentation.
2. *Lack of clear organization and leadership.* Your speech
   isn't structured and doesn't flow logically from one
   point to another.
3. *Too much information.* You overload your audience with
   details, some of them technical and most of them unnecessary.
4. *Not enough support for your ideas, concepts, and information.* You have compelling arguments to make,

but you don't back your ideas up with colorful, memorable stories and examples.

5. *Monotonous voice and sloppy speech.* You believe in your subject and are excited by it, but your voice and manner of speech don't express what you're feeling.

6. *Not meeting the real needs of your audience.* You focus on what interests you, rather than on what your audience is interested in hearing.

These faults are closely linked; improve in one area and you almost automatically improve in the next. Of course, it takes patience and practice to truly hone your speaking abilities, but recognizing and eliminating these six major speaking faults will give you a competitive edge and improve your speaking abilities 100 percent!

The Cardinal Rule: Never Be Boring

This book is also imbued with a rule central to any speaker's success: Never be boring. An audience will forgive almost anything if you don't bore them to death. As a speaker your first job is to be interesting; that's where you generate power: *You* are effective to the degree you capture your *audience*. If you are interesting, entertaining, memorable, then people will think of you as a powerful speaker.

The PowerSpeak system is a strategic shortcut gleaned from years of listening to and training speakers; chapters, exercises, and checklists that cover all the fine points of presenting; and a belief that power will stem from speeches that work hard to keep audiences entertained and interested. These elements make up an effective whole, as I'm sure you will see as you put the PowerSpeak system to work for you. This book was written with three key words—*never be boring*—as the secret weapon that should be in the back of every speaker's mind.

Gaining the Public-Speaking Edge

Confidence and speaking ability go hand in hand. The more speaking you do, the more confident you become—not only of your ability to present but also of your overall corporate skills. When you overcome your fears more easily, you have the ability to truly *persuade* superiors, peers, or customers.

So how do you gain the public-speaking edge? By treating every speaking opportunity as just that—a valuable chance to inform and persuade effectively and thus shape the way you are perceived. This book will teach you how to bring to any meeting or conversation the tools of a powerful speaker's trade: preparation, organization, focus, relevance, enough support for your ideas, and attention to the needs of your audience, whatever the size.

This careful approach to public speaking is tactical; it is designed for you to control your public-speaking situations, rather than vice versa. People who control the effectiveness of spoken communication don't just exhibit confidence; they are also seen as leaders by people who do not grasp the fine points of persuasion. The ability to speak and present clearly, persuasively, and memorably is a skill that will pay off for years to come.

So read on, and start to look at your workday differently—not as a series of random conversations but as myriad chances to polish your skills as a powerful public speaker. The first thing to tackle is fear of public speaking, which the next chapter covers in depth. With fear behind you, you will be free to reap the benefits enjoyed by commanding speakers.

2

Breaking the Fear Barrier

The only thing we have to fear is fear itself.
— Franklin Delano Roosevelt

At a personal and professional growth clinic I once ran, I worked closely with the meeting planners to determine the interests and needs of my audience. My group was concerned about increasing their power within their organizations, but they also indicated they did *not* want me to spend a lot of time on public speaking. I held a discussion on it anyway and had the participants deliver presentations. At the end of the clinic, the evaluations indicated that public speaking was the most valuable segment of all. Some participants confessed the reason they didn't want to see it covered was fear—of public speaking.

According to *The Book of Lists*, public speaking—not bugs, heights, deep water, or even death—is the foremost fear in the world. Roscoe Drummond echoed the feelings of many when he observed, "The mind is a wonderful thing—it starts working the minute you're born and never stops until you get up to speak in public."

What are we so afraid of? What can a room full of people sitting quietly in their chairs—presumably unarmed—do to a speaker? Understanding why facing an audience inspires such fear is the first step toward controlling it.

The Origins of Public-Speaking Panic

It's Lonely in the Spotlight

As a speaker, you're a person apart from the crowd. People are more comfortable in groups than leading them; that way, no one is on the spot, and others can carry the conversation if you run out of ideas. Speaking isolates you; it removes you from your peers and designates you different from everyone else—you're the one who has something worthwhile to say. Some people relish this attention; others, understandably, find the sudden spotlight daunting. The trick is to accept your being singled out; it's temporary, and it's probably an honor, too. So try to see it as an honor, since your perception of the event will be crucial to your success.

It also helps if you don't let the spotlight become a barrier. Many novice speakers blow up their isolation in their own mind, until it takes on exaggerated importance. Think less about yourself and more about your audience and some of the fear will leave, as you perceive yourself not as isolated but as part of the group you're addressing—a group that *wants* to hear what you have to say.

How Am I Doing? (It's Hard to Tell)

Except for optional question-and-answer sessions, speaking is a one-way street. You don't get the direct feedback conversation provides. You're not sure if people are really following you. You can see their eyes—though not very well—but you don't know what they're thinking. A person may leave the room, and you feel personally rejected, even though he is only stepping outside to make a phone call. A joke you've told many times with great success may not get a laugh.

What's missing is swift feedback and knowledge of where you stand, and the absence of this throws you off.

Everyone, not just speakers, needs feedback. To prove this point, a man in a pub took bets from people in the pub and challenged one of England's champion dart throwers that he could make the expert falter in less than four throws—and without interfering with the throw itself. The challenger held up a piece of paper in front of the champion just after he released the dart—so the champion could not see how he did—and then removed the dart before the next throw. Sure enough, the champion's game went to pieces in three throws. Without seeing—instantly—the results of each throw, he missed the next shots.

People do get reactions to their speeches—afterward. Knowing that during the speech you will plunge ahead like the dart thrower, without feedback, accounts for much of the nervousness speakers feel. But forewarned is indeed forearmed. *Expect* the pauses, the small silences, and they won't seem strange. Different audiences will also react differently; don't expect the same noises from both a general audience and one with a very technical bent. And don't misread reactions out of sheer nervousness. Silence can indicate deep thought and agreement as much as it can alert you to boredom.

I once saw a speaker address a small group in a U-shaped seating arrangement. At the back of the room, a man seemed to be paying no attention; he spent the entire speech scribbling and gazing into space. During the break, other people in the audience asked the speaker how he could tolerate the noticeably rude man. The speaker was relaxed; he said he just focused on the rest of the seemingly more interested audience. But after the session was over, the scribbler came up to the speaker, identified himself as a reporter, said he was particularly fascinated by the presentation and would be writing an article on it, and thanked the speaker. Moral: Don't guess at what your audience's reactions mean. It detracts from your effectiveness to worry about those who don't seem to be listening, since they may be listening the hardest, anyway.

I Don't Have the Gift

When I tell someone they can learn to be a commanding speaker, I usually get a swift, standard protest: "But you can't learn it; public speaking is a talent you are either born with or not." Not so. Public speaking is not an innate skill; good speakers are *made*—not born—through hard work and practice. As with any learned skill, some people are better than others, but everyone can work at it successfully.

If someone had told me twenty years ago that I, with my wispy voice and fear of crowds, would really enjoy public speaking, I would not have believed a word. But it's true; and one of the most important kinds of power speaking brings you is the power to change your own perceptions of yourself—not to mention other people's perceptions of you.

Giving a speech is not a natural, ordinary event. Speakers who expect to feel at ease are kidding themselves. It may seem hard to believe that even the most polished, experienced speakers get nervous, but they do. So don't expect, or long for, relaxation; expect the nervous excitement and energy that come from the task at hand. In other words, use fear to your advantage; charisma and adrenaline are closely linked.

Making Fear Work for You

Fear is nature's way of helping you protect yourself. New or dangerous situations trigger the "fight or flight" response: Your pulse quickens, your muscles tense, and the resulting rush of adrenaline equips you for any extra effort you might need. Whether you face real or imaginary fear, physical danger, or emotional stress, the reaction is the same. And speakers benefit: The adrenaline becomes energy; their minds seem more alert; new thoughts, facts, and ideas arise. In fact, some of my best ad libs come to me in front of my toughest audiences; it's yet another gift from the adrenaline.

Nervousness can give your speech the edge—and the passion—all good speeches need. It has always been so; two thousand years ago Cicero said all public speaking of real merit was characterized by nervousness. But how can you draw the line between nervousness that boosts and fear that debilitates? By understanding and tackling the three fears shared by all speakers:

- Fear of performing poorly
- Fear of the audience
- Fear your material is not good enough

Overcoming the Three Fears of Public Speaking

Fear of Performing Poorly

You are not alone. Worrying about your performance comes with the territory. It haunts novice and experienced performers alike: Even after fifty years of acting, Helen Hayes worried she would forget her opening lines. Comedian Red Skelton was always a nervous wreck before performances.

Even the most practiced public speakers do battle with nerves; it's a sign you're a true speaker. One night at a convention, a woman entered a room and saw the evening's keynote speaker pacing frantically. She asked him why he was so nervous. "What do you mean? Who's nervous?" he demanded. "If you're not nervous," she replied, "What are you doing in the ladies' room?"

The Power of Privacy. Speaking before a group may seem like the most public act possible, but you still have privacy on your side. You don't have to reveal your nervousness; you can keep it to yourself. You gain nothing by letting others know you're worried; if you act confident, you begin to feel that way, too. People rarely *look* very nervous, no matter how jittery they feel.

In my public-speaking classes, 95 percent of the people are amazed when they see videotapes of themselves giving a speech. They don't see on the screen the nervousness they felt. But they have to believe the camera and believe in an audience's positive response. Letting go of the fear means realizing it doesn't matter if you feel nervous; the audience doesn't know how nervous you are and won't be able to see it either.

Keep in mind the example of the frightened boy walking past the cemetery on a dark night. As long as he walked casually and whistled gaily he was fine. When he decided to walk faster, he could not resist the temptation to run; and when he ran, terror took over. It's the same with public speaking: Don't take that first fast step. Don't give in, don't show fear, and don't talk about your fear.

Tap into Creative Visualization.   Expectations have a way of fulfilling themselves. If you assume your audience is hostile, you will adopt a defensive and abrupt manner, which is sure to alienate some people. Instead, form a mental image of how you want to look: *Creative visualization* is a technique that works for many public speakers and performers. Close your eyes and remember the positive points and audience rapport from your last speech. Imagine an audience of friendly, accepting people. Substitute that vision as the reality in your mind's eye and keep it there. Visualization is also a good way to try out new jokes or openings you are afraid to use: Imagine a positive audience reaction, and you're halfway to getting just that.

Greg Louganis, the great Olympic diver, always visualizes a perfect dive, even if he doesn't take off from the board's ''sweet spot,'' the area on a board that gives a diver an advantage if he hits it when he dives. Louganis takes what he gets and makes it perfect nonetheless. Gold medals are the result. The key to a good speech is *envi-*

sioning that you are hitting a sweet spot, even if everything isn't going perfectly, and even if you are nervous. When I speak, I envision myself *totally* in control—a gracious, charming, warm, and enthusiastic presenter. The key to visualization is controlling the mental image of yourself; don't let what you think the audience is thinking affect your image of yourself.

Envision the role you want to play and act the part. Don't worry about seeming phony—we all have many sides to our characters. You want to show your confident side; it is there for you to tap. With practice, confidence becomes natural and comfortable, and visualization is a powerful tool for gaining that confidence.

Work with Your Body. Just as visualization works as a mental aid for speakers, these three exercises help you feel better physically:

1. *Proper breathing.* Concentrate on deep nasal breathing using your diaphragm. Breathe through your nose so you don't make your mouth dry.
2. *Progressive relaxation.* Working up from your feet, tense different parts of your body and then relax them. You'll lose much of that clamminess and nervousness.
3. *Easing neck strain.* Roll your head in a circle from shoulder to shoulder, as if you were a limp rag doll. This relaxes your throat and vocal cords.

You can do most of these exercises right on the dais (at least the first two). No need to resort to bathroom pacing.

Confidence Cards. Aptly named, these notecards help speakers by ordering information, including all the points the speaker wants to make. They bring a sense of control to what often seems like an unwieldy situation. Chapter 20 ("Delivering with Style") will detail how to add to your confidence by using notecards.

Fear of the Audience

Audiences are not out to get you. In fact, your listeners want you to do well and are probably thrilled that it's you up there and not them. They want to put themselves in your hands, listen, and learn. And they listen best when you appear confident and in control. Great speakers convince the audience they are completely in control, no matter how nervous they may really be. It's difficult for an audience to relax if the speaker appears uncomfortable; appear confident and you're already winning its appreciation.

I attended a standing-room-only conference on stage fright where Frederick Zlotkin, first cellist for the New York City Ballet Orchestra, pointed out that how we perceive the audience affects our degree of fear and nervousness. He divides those perceptions into three kinds of anxiety: low range, medium range, and high range. Low-range speakers are slightly nervous but perceive the audience as basically neutral. Medium-range speakers assume negative thoughts on the part of the audience and consequently block out their listeners. They hide behind their lecterns and avoid eye contact. High-range speakers extend this mistake further and actually experience the audience as hostile, waiting for them to make a mistake.

Identify with Your Listeners.   In each of the above cases, the audience is the same and the differences are in the speaker's mind. One way to avoid this me-versus-them trap is to think about your audience instead of yourself. The more you know about your listeners, the more you will see them as friends and the less nervous you will be. What are their backgrounds, interests, needs? How will they benefit by hearing you? They want to enjoy listening to you; how can you make that happen?

Give Passion a Place.   My daughter Laura is not a public speaker, but she talks with total confidence to groups of three hundred people about the importance of self-defense. She says she's so excited about her subject and about helping her audience learn to defend itself that she doesn't even think about being nervous.

Communicate Your Excitement.   Focus on *wanting* to tell your listeners something—something you feel is really worth your time and theirs. That kind of excitement is contagious; your audience can't help but catch it. And concentrating on teaching your audience something vital gets you thinking more about it than about yourself—the perfect antidote to fear.

Remember Who the Expert Is.   A final note on audience fear: Remember the facts. You were invited to speak. You're supposed to know more about your subject than the audience; you are there because you are more capable of covering the subject than most people. Believe it. As Broadway star Ethel Merman used to say: "If the audience could perform better than I can, *they'd* be up here on stage singing."

Fear Your Material Is Not Good Enough

This is the easiest fear to overcome because you are in control of preparation and content. You won't be on the spot if you know your subject thoroughly.

Construct your Speech with Care.   Do your homework. Research. Prepare. The more thorough your preparations, the more you will be convinced the material *is* good enough. Work and rework your speech until you know it is interesting, worthwhile, and meaningful to the audience. Then edit it. All good writers will tell you there is no such thing as good writing—only rewriting.

Other chapters in this book will cover the organization

and preparation of your speech. But planning is only half the battle; practicing your delivery is the other.

Fear of New Material. Experienced speakers are often afraid to try something new: to change an opening that has always worked, to add new material that hasn't been tested. As scary as public speaking may seem, it's important to take additional risks. The first time I had to give physical directions to an audience, I was very nervous; my presentation required that at one point I ask everyone to move to the sides of the room. I panicked. What if no one moved? But I went ahead and there were no problems. Don't let fear keep you from trying something new to improve your presentations.

Practice Can Make Perfect. Artur Rubenstein, the great pianist, used to say, "If I don't practice for one day, I know it; if I don't practice for two days, my critics know it; and if I miss three days—the audience knows it."

Practice until you are 100-percent confident. One hour for every minute of your speech is a good rule of thumb. Practice in different settings, at different times, testing different presentation techniques. Practice in front of a mirror, into a tape recorder, for a group of friends—anyone who will take the time to listen to you.

Even with all your practicing, keep the speech or presentation fresh. After two thousand performances of *Othello*, Sir Laurence Olivier forgot his lines. He felt it was God's way of keeping him anxious. Every speech, no matter how many times you deliver it, should sound fresh.

Of course, the best kind of practice is public speaking itself; the more you do, the better you become. But don't be misled by unrealistically high expectations. Public speaking is an art that only improves with time. Keep at it. You may still be nervous, but you'll also be better.

Mind over Fear

Fear may not be welcome, but it is normal. Every successful speaker has his or her own tricks to *psych out* fear. Winston Churchill liked to imagine that each member of the audience was naked. Franklin Roosevelt pretended that the members all had holes in their socks. Carol Burnett thinks of them sitting on the commode. The point is, even though your mind seems to work overtime before a speech, filling you with dread, you can counter with tricks of the imagination that make you feel confident and in control.

The Best Tip of Them All: Confidence

Fear has its good side: The perception of public speaking as difficult and demanding adds to a confident speaker's power, since people are perceived as more knowledgeable and confident simply because of their ability to conquer the dreaded task of public speaking. That confidence comes from within; once you believe you have the ability to be a confident speaker, it's a lot easier to be just that.

The best way to bolster your confidence before a speech or presentation is to *think positively*. Saturate your mind with positive thoughts. Repeat to yourself any positive catch phrase that appeals: "I am poised, prepared, persuasive, positive, and powerful. I also feel composed, confident, convincing, commanding, and compelling."

Keys to Breaking the Fear Barrier

- Admit your fear; understand its sources.
- Tap the energy that fear produces.
- Recognize that fear is normal for public speakers.
- Realize your fear doesn't have to show.
- Visualize yourself as a powerful speaker.
- See the audience as your ally; focus on its needs.

- Speak about something you care about.
- Combine preparation with practice.
- Devise tricks to psych out your fear.
- Think positively about yourself.

By keeping these steps in mind, you can put fear in its place and get on with the career-enhancing opportunities that await you by becoming an excellent and persuasive public speaker.

Professional Project: Work On Your Fear

Decide on your personal action plan for controlling your fear. Write it on an index card and study it before each presentation.

3

Preparation: The Source

of a Speaker's Power

*The will to win is nothing, unless you have the will to
prepare.*   —Anonymous

Of all the ways to banish fear—and the previous chapter
revealed a whole host of them—one stands out: simple,
thorough preparation. For the unprepared speaker the terror is real; it's a feeling all too close to everyone's classic
nightmare where it's exam time and you didn't go to class
all term. . . .

But the prepared speaker knows no such terror. He or
she realizes preparation is the foundation, the blueprint,
for a successful speech. There is an old saying that a
speech well prepared is nine-tenths delivered. That's a statistic that really puts fear in its place and leaves you ready
to deliver a polished performance.

I used to audition on Broadway, and at first, it was a
terrifying experience. But after six months of practicing,
auditions became something I looked forward to, once I
learned how to prepare for them.

Audiences Sense Preparation

Preparation ensures that your audience will never be in
doubt about what you are trying to say—and neither will
you. Careful preparation sharpens your perceptions and
gives you great confidence. The more homework you do,

the more spontaneous, confident, and relaxed you are
when you deliver the speech.

Preparation As Process

How do you prepare? The traditional answer—taking notes
and memorizing them—is just a small part of it. Real preparation means digging something out of yourself; it means
gathering and arranging your thoughts, nurturing your
ideas, and finding a unique way to express them. A speech
needs time to grow; don't try to manufacture one in a
hurry. Select your topic as soon as you can but don't rush
to write down your speech. Start a speech file as soon as
you know you will be speaking and put everything that
comes to mind in this file: thoughts, quotations, topics.
Let the thinking process go on for a long time—at least
two or three weeks—depending on your subject and the
length of the speech. Sleep on it; dream about it. Let your
ideas sink into your subconscious.

Then bring your evolving speech out of hiding. Make it
a topic of conversation at the dinner table. Ask yourself
questions about your topic. Write down your thoughts and
the examples that come to you. Once you have the pot
cooking, keep stirring it and adding new ideas and illustrations. Examples will pop into your head at random
times—at the bus stop, while driving your car. Jot down
as many of these inspirations as you can.

Brood with the Best of Them

As you brood, you will be in good historical company.
Abraham Lincoln was known to brood on a speech for
days or weeks. He carried little notes to himself in his hat.
Eventually he arranged these jottings in order, wrote, re-
vised, and shaped his speeches. But up until that last moment, he pondered and polished. On the Sunday before

he was to deliver the speech dedicating the Gettysburg cemetery he told a friend that the speech wasn't exactly finished. "I have written it over two or three times," he said, "and I shall have to give it another lick before I am satisfied."

The night before, he closeted himself away from the crowds and practiced his speech. He worked on it all night and was still absorbed in thought as he rode to the cemetery. When the moment came, he delivered the nation's most celebrated 266 words in less than five minutes.

After you've applied the Lincoln method and let your topic simmer in your mind, your next step is to actually prepare your talk, step by step. The order of the steps is also important, because it addresses your concerns in the order they arise. By themselves, the steps are easy to tackle. They take the daunting task of doing a speech from scratch and make it manageable, even fun.

The Thirteen Easy Steps to Preparation

1. Think about the purpose of the speech. Is the purpose of your talk to inform, to entertain, to persuade, or to call your audience to action? Every speech must have its own topic and reason for being.

2. Analyze the audience. A gossip is one who talks to you about others; a bore is one who talks to you about himself; and a brilliant conversationalist is one who talks to you about yourself. Speak *to* your audience; know its members and understand their interests, attitudes, goals, and fears. Speak to what they know and care about, and you are on your way to a memorable speech. Chapter 9 goes into this crucial step in detail.

3. Gather enough material. Start by collecting all your thoughts and notes. After you have exhausted your thinking on your topic, go to the library and research. Imitate the great journalists—they never use most of their research, but doing research gives them a reserve they can draw on. It makes them more expert in their topics than before they began.

Take advantage of trade publications and associations—two excellent sources of industry-specific information. I once gave a speech to the members of the American Lung Association. I researched the association and its concerns so thoroughly that people listening to the speech thought I was on the staff of the association. That's the fun of preparation—learning enough so that you really communicate with your audience, while adding to your own knowledge as well.

Then be ready and willing to discard the unnecessary facts. Select only information relevant to your audience and to this particular speech. Your task is not to elaborate but to simplify and reinforce.

4. Compose one concise sentence that clearly states your purpose. This will become your focus—or even your title—and as you put the rest of your speech together you will constantly refer back to this one line that will keep you on target.

5. Construct an outline. Would you build a building without a foundation? You couldn't; and you also can't build your speech until you lay its foundation, which is the outline. In the outline you will reduce your ideas to three or four main sentences or key phrases and arrange them in the most convincing order. Chapter 5 will give you outlining ideas.

6. Add support. Now you will fill out the outline by adding explanations, support, facts, anecdotes, and stories to give depth and meaning to your main points. As a rule of thumb, you can spend 5 percent of your time defining the purpose and mood of your speech, 10 percent of your time outlining, another 10 percent on visuals, and 25 percent practicing.

That leaves 50 percent of your time to spend on working

on the support that colors your speech and brings it to life. Your mood could be serious, jovial, or closely tied with concerns facing the audience. Whatever the mood, the support you choose must reinforce the mood you have chosen and ensure that your speech is never boring. Although it's easy to gather facts, they don't make an interesting speech by themselves.

7. Prepare all visual aids. If your speech needs visual aids, fine; if you don't need them, or your material does not lend itself to them, then don't try to fit them in.

If used properly, visual aids can be effective. People remember 40 percent more when they hear *and* see something simultaneously. But remember that visual aids can be simple: I remember a salesman giving a speech suddenly holding up a shoe with a large hole for the audience to see. He made his point about the necessity of pounding the pavement—and memorably, too. Visual aids are covered in detail in chapter 16.

8. Devise an opening with impact. It may be humorous, surprising, informative, challenging—an opening can be anything original that works for your particular speech. You make your first impression in the introduction; it can cloud all that follows or assure people that what follows is worth listening closely to.

In business presentations, it's important to tell your audience what's coming up. But you have to do this without losing its attention. Refrain from sentences that start out "I'm Jane Jones, VP of marketing. Today I'll be covering . . ." It's dull.

It's much better to get your audience's attention first and *then* explain your purpose. Jane Jones could start her talk on the benefits of exercise by saying: "Good morning, I'm Jane Jones and I'll be talking to you today about why exercise is important for executives, no matter how busy you are." Or she could grab her audience: "Did you know that twenty minutes of exercise three times a week can add ten years to your life? Good morning, I'm Jane Jones, and after my talk you'll be able to walk out of here ready to begin a sound exercise program.''

Refrain from saving major surprises for the end, and grab people with the facts—and your focus—early on.

9. Craft your conclusion. Build up to it, even if you are ending by summarizing your main points. Then end the speech with a strong, dynamic challenge that tells the members of the audience what you expect them to do with the information you've given them. Conclusions, like openings, must be memorable.

10. Write your speech, polish it, and edit it. Put it aside for a day or two, then go back and rewrite any parts you think need it. Remember Lincoln and his need to tinker. One way to achieve his admirable conciseness is to edit—ruthlessly. Don't be afraid to cut one-third—or even one-half—of your prose; this will leave you with a text that is stronger, leaner, and clearer. Technical presenters in particular are prone to excess words. Distill your speech down to the essentials, especially if it is technical, so it will be easier for your audience to follow. Don't be afraid of being brief and clear—too few speakers are.

Effective written communication is different from its oral counterpart. A speech is a temporary event—words float in the air and are gone. Your words will have a better chance of staying with your audience if you take advantage of oral communication's greater informality: Use short sentences and words, colorful language, sentence fragments, contractions, repetition, and questions. All of these work to make your words lively and memorable.

And finally, once you are satisfied, practice your delivery.

11. Get your timing down. Part of practicing your delivery is timing your speech. We speak approximately 150 words a minute, so three double-spaced typewritten pages take five minutes to deliver, depending on how quickly you speak.

Even though you can never time a speech to the precise second, there is no substitute for recording your speech and estimating the time. If you have a lot of jokes, stories, and audience questions, you'll have to allow extra time for them.

When it comes time to deliver the speech, keep a digital clock or a watch on the lectern where you can see it easily, or have somebody in the audience signal you when you have five minutes left. As you approach these final five minutes, you'll know you have just enough time left to finish an important point before going into your closing statement or before asking for questions.

12. Get off on the right foot: Write your own introduction. Your introduction is the first thing your audience hears about you and your first chance to make an impression. Professional speakers known for a personal style don't leave these crucial first words in the hands of others. An introduction you write yourself (for someone else to deliver) warms up the audience, lists appropriate qualifications, and acts as a bridge that lets you cross over directly into your speech. And you know it will be accurate. Many a speaker has had to begin a speech by correcting a biographical flaw in an introduction written by someone who did not check the facts too carefully.

There are still risks when you write your own introduction—someone may mess up the humor you're trying to insert, or mispronounce something—but you reduce the chance of mistakes if you provide the text yourself.

Always send your introduction in advance with a note saying that it ties into your speech and should be read as is. You can leave some space for your presenter to add something if he or she wishes; just indicate the best place for this. Type the introduction in caps and double-space it so it's easy to read. Make it short and to the point. It should include these four points and not much more: your name and title, your qualifications, why the speech can benefit the audience, and why you've been asked to speak.

When you list your qualifications, name only the best three or four examples, or the ones that pertain to that particular audience.

Here's a sample self-introduction written by Joel Weldon, a well-known speaker.

> Our speaker this morning is Joel Weldon. His subject is titled, ''Elephants Don't Bite: It's the Little Things That Get You.'' Joel comes to us from Scottsdale, Arizona, where he heads up his own personal development company. In the past six years, he has conducted over 1,000 seminars and workshops for some of America's top organizations.
>
> The reason we have him here today is because of his unique ability to help successful speakers become even more successful. He's creative and fun to listen to. And his unusual business card tells you, ''Success comes in cans, not in cannots.'' Speaking on ''Elephants Don't Bite: It's the Little Things That Get You,'' help me welcome Joel Weldon.*

That's an introduction that does a lot: It's short, simple, and vivid.

I always close my self-introductions with a pleasant touch I learned from some Southern hosts: ''Please join me in welcoming Dorothy Leeds and PowerSpeak.'' Ending with a comment like that always brings a nice round of applause, which gives you support as you approach the platform.

13. Make a last-minute checklist. A key aspect of preparation is controlling and preparing your speaking environment. Avoid last-minute problems by making sure you take care of all the little details—like arranging chairs in a small

---

*Printed material given out during ''Elephants Don't Bite'' (''Doing the Little Things as a Speaker That Will Get Big Results''), presented at the 1981 National Speakers Association Convention, July 28, 1981, by Joel Weldon. Copyright 1981 by Joel H. Weldon & Associates, Inc.

gathering and clearing away empty cups—before the speech. Other details to attend to before you speak can include:

▣ Deciding what you're going to wear.
▣ Making two copies of your text or notes.
▣ Bringing your glasses.
▣ Knowing if you'll have a podium.
▣ Preparing visual-aids equipment and lighting.

Lists compiled by truly prepared speakers are exhaustive and call attention to another crucial aspect of preparation: stage managing—overseeing all the details of your speech that don't have to do with your words. Chapter 17 will give you all the information you need on the key tasks that make up stage managing.

Preparation Knows No Shortcuts

These thirteen steps constitute the ultimate outline for a person giving a speech. Sure, you can skip one, or cut a few corners, but the audience will notice. Every *minute* of your presentation should be supported by an *hour* of preparation time. It's also important to prepare for your general communications: talking to your boss about a raise or presenting something to a client. Even a telephone call requires preplanning: You should know what you plan to cover and what your objectives are.

Without preparing sufficiently, the odds are you will commit one of the six major speaking faults, which are explained in depth in the next six chapters. Tackle each step in order and you will have the foundation for a memorable speech.

Here's a summary in the form of questions you can ask yourself:

- In one concise sentence, what is the purpose behind this speech?
- Who is the audience and what is its main interest in this topic?
- What do I already know and believe about this topic as it relates to this audience? What additional research can I do?
- What are the main points of my outline?
- What supporting information and stories can I use to support each of these main points?
- What visual aids—if any—do I need?
- Do I have an arresting opening?
- In my final summary, have I explained to those in the audience what I expect them to do with this information?
- Have I polished and practiced the language of the speech to the best of my ability?
- Have I written a concise introduction for myself?
- Have I taken care of all the little details that will help me speak confidently?

With fear put into perspective and with the foundation of preparation under you, you're ready to start eliminating the six major faults that get in the way of powerful speeches, and the next six chapters will show you how.

Professional Project: Build Confidence Through Preparation

Go through the questions above. Note first your strengths in preparation and then the aspects of issues you tend to avoid. What are you going to do about them?

Part II

How to Overcome the Six Major Speaking Faults and Shine as a Public Speaker

4

Fault #1:

An Unclear Purpose

During the course of most speeches, the audience, as a rule, can figure out what the speech's subject is, but not the object.
                                                                —Anonymous

A well-thought out purpose is so elemental it's often overlooked. Have you ever sat in an audience and asked yourself when the speaker was going to get to the point? Or heard a speech just drift—along with the audience? The subject may be compelling, the speaker even charismatic, but without determining a clear purpose, the speaker fails to lead the audience.

In front of an audience, speakers are leaders—in charge of moving that audience from one point to another. And you can only be a leader—and attain the power that goes with leadership—if you have a clear purpose in mind. No one should be in doubt for long as to your purpose unless you're saving some shock for the end, and even then, you had better make sure your audience can follow along.

The purpose of your speech is what you want to leave in the minds of those in your audience and what you want them to do as a result of hearing you. Many speakers confuse purpose with title or subject. In fact, every talk needs all three: a title, a subject, and a purpose. For example:

Title: "Buckle Up and Live Longer"
Subject: Automotive safety
Purpose: To make more people wear seat belts

33

How to Determine Your Purpose

You can zero in on your purpose by asking: What do I want to accomplish in the minds of those in my audience? What do I want them to do, feel, or know?

Knowing clearly how you want the members of your audience to feel will affect the mood of your speech, your choice of examples and stories, how you build the argument: Every element is influenced by the effect of your overall purpose.

Start by Stating Your Purpose

It can be surprisingly tough to set down a clear-cut statement of your purpose. In my public-speaking classes I always ask people to state their purpose; usually the speaker is not too clear on this, even after giving a speech. That doubt can stem from an attempt to convey too much, to make sure an audience gets all the facts. Don't be an overloaded speaker who drifts and at the end can't get back to the original topic. With your purpose defined at the outset, you can make sure all that follows supports your aims and that no one ends up wondering what point you were trying to get across.

How do you do this? The first step is to figure out which type of purpose yours is. Will you be speaking to entertain or to impart information? Or do you need to go beyond informing and actually convince, or even rouse your audience to action? It's quite possible your purpose will involve a combination of these goals. If it does, which one is paramount?

A good purpose is a specific one. Your general purpose may be to inform, but you must focus on exactly what you are going to get across. Do you get loads of mail on executive seminars? Look at the descriptions of courses offered: Each objective is spelled out clearly. Speaking of this book, I could say my purpose is to teach you about public speaking, but that's vague. It would be more specific to say I want to teach you how to be a powerful speaker by avoiding the six major speaking faults.

Don't Let Your Subject Swallow You

When the purpose gets too broad, it gets confused with the *subject*. Keep these two separate and you're well on your way to focusing your talk. You may have to speak on "Corporate Leadership in the 80s"; if you think of that as the purpose of your talk, any panic is justified. A topic like that is just a broad subject; your purpose is to make a specific point about leadership—maybe even in a specific company—through examples, anecdotes, and various facts. So tackle some key trees, not the whole forest. Your purpose in such a speech could be to inform the audience of the skills necessary to achieve leadership in a corporation. Or it could be to convince people to start preparing now for changing leadership roles in the 1990s. The possibilities in the subject are vast, so you must be very clear and specific about your purpose.

The more focused and specific your talk, the better your chances that some words will resonate. Speak vividly about the leadership of one person, and your audience can glean much about leadership in general. Let people make the leap from the specific to the general, while you continue to be vivid. Broad subjects can be wonderful assignments if you give them a narrow—and therefore memorable—purpose and focus.

Analyze the Audience

Always ask yourself how the purpose of your talk relates to your audience's interests. Knowing your audience is the only way to understand its attitudes and anticipate its objections. A dentist addressing a group of parents would talk about preventing tooth decay in their children, not about the latest equipment installed in his office. Study those in your audience; think of their needs. You must link the beliefs you are trying to impart with their existing concerns. Chapter 9 ("Not Meeting the Real Needs of Your Audience") goes into this crucial analysis in detail.

Let Purpose Lead the Argument

If you titled your leadership speech "A Group Without a Leader Is Like a Boat Without a Rudder," that title would lead naturally into your general purpose—to get those in your audience to act, to change their behavior, and adopt and use the five leadership strategies you are about to introduce. You could go on to support your purpose by explaining what could happen if they don't use them and what will happen if they do.

Get Mileage Out of Your Title

Many speakers either omit their title altogether or tack on something at the last minute. But your title is the first thing about your speech an audience sees or hears, and it deserves a lot of care. Good speakers use titles as part of their strategy; nothing communicates creativity quicker than a well-worded title. A lively title will also help the meeting planner, who frequently will print them on whatever he or she is using to summarize or sell the meeting.

A weak title is better than no title at all—barely. Compare "Safety" to "Be Safe and Live Longer: Ten Steps to a Healthy Workplace" and "Managing Well" to "How to Be a Super Boss."

Always use titles—even for a meeting you're running in your own corporation. It's your first chance to catch your audience's attention.

Fine-Tune Your Tone

Establishing your purpose is the beginning of the fine-tuning all good speakers do. And the same purpose can lend itself to talks with very different thrusts, depending on your audience. For example, a talk on leadership to senior executives will differ from one to new managers. The thrust may change from reinforcing to introducing; the examples relevant to the audience's business life will be different. Other shifts would occur if you prepared a talk on the same topic to laypeople and technical experts.

Should speeches be entertaining, strictly technical, or a little of both? Speeches have their own *tenors* that can either be inappropriate to the subject at hand or just right. The twist you put on the facts will guide much of your audience's reaction to the information you're imparting.

A plea for humor: Even if your purpose and your tone are extremely serious, you shouldn't neglect the saving grace of humor. An amusing example or story is still one of the best ways to be memorable; even Shakespeare had comedy in the midst of his most tragic plays. I am not suggesting you work at being a stand-up comic but that you take advantage of the bond created when speakers get audiences to laugh with them.

Don't Just Inform. . . . Persuade!

Alas, the speaker's task is seldom as simple as imparting information. Granted, informing is central to the job; speaking is an efficient way of conveying timely information to large groups. But chances are your objectives as a speaker are to *persuade*, to give your audience new information in such a way that it sees things your way. This is the purpose behind the purpose, the end result that speakers seek.

You can see these two goals—informing and persuading—at work in business and technical presentations, where the topics, the facts, and the statistics are presented with a clear objective in sight: to win that account, reorganize that department, revamp that computer system. As tools of persuasion, speeches and presentations are everyday events. But it's not enough to be clear, you need to be compelling, too.

I once heard a principal speak to the parents of his students about drunk driving, a subject of such inherent seriousness that he should have been able to lead the parents with ease. But he never made his purpose clear: His facts and presentation were jumbled; his stories weren't focused; and up until the very end, the parents were left wondering what the point was.

In fact, he had a very specific point: He wanted the audience to write letters to the legislature supporting tougher laws. But since he waited until the last few sentences to spring this request on them—instead of weaving the effect concerned citizens can have throughout his talk—his audience felt more put upon than activated.

He made the mistake of thinking that informing is the same as motivating. It's not. Informing is a preliminary step to getting people to act, but facts need support, organization, and clear communication of benefits to get results from an audience.

Compel Through Commitment

The key to being compelling lies in your own commitment to, and fondness for, your topic. And it comes from knowing exactly what you want to say. Sound familiar? We're back to the original task of defining your purpose—knowing what you want to say. But that second step—persuading—needs a commitment from you to your topic. Funny stories, slides, and startling statistics all may help you make your case, but your own commitment as a speaker—the passion and the tangible belief that you can summon—is hard to beat when you combine it with a logical, informative presentation.

To be the excited—and exciting—kind of speaker people remember, you must believe in your material. This is especially true when your purpose is to convince or motivate. Your enthusiasm must be genuine and palpable; anything contrived will seem just that.

Was Your Purpose Clear? Get Feedback

Get in the habit of asking people who have heard you whether your purpose was clear. Before you give your next talk or chair a meeting, write a sentence that you feel describes your purpose. After you deliver your presentation, ask the participants what your purpose was. They should be able to tell you—easily. See how closely what they say matches what you wrote. If it doesn't, you need to work harder on making the content support and evoke the purpose you have in mind. Without feedback, you can only assume your purpose was clear—you'll never know for sure.

Focused, committed, invigorated—isn't that the kind of speaker you enjoy hearing? It is the kind you can become, and the first step is that firm grasp of purpose. Determining your purpose really is an easy step, and it makes everything that follows, including organization and selecting good supporting material, much easier. When you communicate a strong purpose people see you as a leader with vision, which can't help but add power to your presentations.

Professional Projects: Concentrate on Purpose

1. Listen to some politicians and see if you can write down a clear, one-sentence summation of the purpose of the speech you are listening to.
2. Think about your next meeting with your boss and clearly write out a purpose that will help keep you focused and assure you of better results.

5

Fault #2: Lack of Clear Organization and Leadership

Properly organized, even crime pays.
—Jim Fisk and Robert Barron

Eliminating the six major speaking faults from your speech is like climbing a ladder: It's a methodical, successive practice; you use each rung to get to the next. Clarifying your own purpose is essential; the next thing to avoid in the climb to a powerful speech is a lack of organization.

A poorly organized speech wreaks havoc with even the most compelling ideas. You could have the most interesting topic and the most willing audience, but if you don't structure the speech, well, it's like slipping suddenly when you discover there's a rung missing on your ladder. You're left dangling and so is your audience. Good organization also helps prevent audience boredom: The people in your audience don't have to wonder where you are going if they see you are proceeding logically. So they remain focused on your ideas and don't get sidetracked. They put themselves in your hands much more willingly if they sense you know where you're going and how you're going to get there.

Outlining: The Secret to Organization

Fine speakers have various methods of approaching their material, but they all have one thing in common: a good outline. It highlights the important elements of your talk, gets rid of the excess, and helps you choose the best supporting information. An outline compels you to analyze your logic and reveals any gaps or flaws in your reasoning.

A strong outline also helps you perform your speech better because you visualize your main points in your mind. Your talk flows easily toward the conclusion without hesitation.

The biggest advantage of a good outline is that it can be modified to meet different situations and demands. With the right outline, you can change a twenty-minute speech into a five-minute one, and vice versa.

Indeed, you should be prepared to deliver long, medium-length, or short versions of your speech, especially if you are the last speaker and the speakers before you ran over their time limits. A British foreign secretary was once at the mercy of a long-winded toastmaster who took up all the remaining time and most of the audience's patience. When the toastmaster finally introduced the secretary with the words ". . . and now our foreign secretary will give his address," the gentleman stood up and said: "I have been asked to give my entire address in the remaining five minutes. That I can do. Here it is: 10 Carlton Gardens, London, England." He then sat down, to appreciative applause.

Avoiding the Endless Outline Trap

The most frequent outline mistake is not making it simple and orderly. You may be tempted to cover many items, which all seem to be equally important. That's an understandable impulse; you don't want to leave out key facts or topics. But this approach will get you in the end. For starters, it's doubtful all those tempting items are equal in importance. And your audience just can't absorb that many points.

So you must establish priorities. First, identify the three or four major points that need to be covered. Then establish subheads that will provide the framework people will use to absorb the information.

A popular management phrase these days is "lean and mean"; think of a good outline as being "lean and clean." The following is a good general outline that should suit most presentations. It's designed to grab your audience, hold its attention, and provide the right amount of information.

Sample PowerSpeak Outline for a Twenty-Minute Presentation

INTRODUCTION: (5 percent of your time)
I.   Opening statement to gain attention and interest— capitalizes on audience's goodwill.
     A. Development of opening statement
     B. Other supporting material if needed
II. Second introductory point (if necessary).

BODY: (90 percent of your time)
III. First main point of your speech.
     A. Major subpoint supporting III
     B. Subpoint supporting III
IV. Second main point of speech.
     A. Major subpoint supporting IV
     B. Subpoint supporting IV
V.   Third main point of speech.
     A. Major subpoint supporting V
     B. Subpoint supporting V

CONCLUSION: (5 percent of your time)
VI. Summary.
    A. Famous last words
    B. Thank the audience
VII. Application and final statement.

The Three Parts That Make Up a Convincing Whole

Your speech will have an introduction, a body, and a conclusion. All three parts are equally important, but the bulk of your talk is taken up by the body of the speech. Many speakers prepare the body first, and then go back to the introduction and conclusion. Prepare your speech in the order that works for you.

Don't Forget Transitions

Transitions are so basic that many speakers overlook them and concentrate on structuring the outline. But transitions get you from one part of the outline to another; they are the secret to a professional's speech. Look at the sample outline above and realize there should be transitions between each main point and subpoint. These devices are so important to organization—and to giving good presentations—that I've devoted all of chapter 11 to them.

After you have written down your three or four key topics, keep track of everything you can think of that supports these main points. Anecdotes, research, clippings, and facts will all be necessary to provide the support—and the color—a memorable speech needs.

PEP: The Formula for Success

Here is an important piece of information that will really aid you in speaking powerfully. And it's so simple to use. For all your major points, do this: Make your point, give a descriptive example, and then *remake* the point as creatively as possible. That's PEP—Point, Example, Point. You're taking advantage of how people learn (through repetition and illustration). Retention is the key to a powerful speech.

My training programs recognize the importance of retention and I turn lessons into games and role playing— vivid, real-life examples of principles that participants will remember far more readily than a dry synposis. The same principle is at work in a speech; since people remember vivid stories and examples, use them to increase the level of what people remember when they listen to you. See chapter 7 for a discussion of building enough support for your speech and the various useful devices at your disposal.

After you have applied the PEP formula and sorted out the various support materials, you may have material left over. If your leftovers won't group around your main points, they are probably irrelevant. Throw them out. Even if they do apply, set them aside, for they will probably make the speech too long. Make it a cardinal rule to stick to your main ideas, and get rid of the clutter. Sometimes these leftovers are handy if you ever need a longer version of your talk. I give fifteen-minute and forty-five-minute talks on the same subject and find the leftovers invaluable. But only if there's a proper place for them.

It's also possible you'll wind up with some important information that doesn't seem to fit under your main points. In this case your main points may not be broad enough. Go back to square one and restate them in a larger framework.

Choosing a Style: Making the Sequence Your Own

Once you've grouped your subheads and examples under the main points, the next crucial job is to work out the *sequence* you will present them in and the *style* that fits your purpose best. Your choice of sequence must build from point to point both to maintain interest and move the speech along. It might be entertaining to string ten jokes together, but if the string doesn't add up to a ball of yarn, the audience is dissatisfied. On the other hand, it may be logical to present a series of facts in chronological order, but that can also be boring.

Select a style of organization, but don't be too predictable. The last thing you want is a complacent audience. In the middle of a presentation I made the mistake of saying, "Let me be more organized." I felt the entire audience deflate—enthusiasm just wilted. So I quickly added, "I said organized, not boring." And the audience perked right up again.

An outline may seem strict and uncompromising by definition, but it's governed by the sequence of your points, and here you are free to create. You can start with small points and build to a climax. Or you can open with an attention-getter, and follow with less startling points. A skilled writer can achieve the same objective a hundred different ways, and as a speaker you can do the same thing. You may organize your points by using contrast and comparison; by moving historically from the most primitive examples to the most modern; or simply by going from the simple to the complex, the smallest to the largest, the cheapest to the most expensive.

Whatever you do, choose a pattern that sells *your* message, fits your own thinking and style, and helps the audience move along with you clearly and logically. And remember to always hold something back for your windup. All speeches should end on a high point.

The Four Classic Organization Patterns

You can present your speech in a limitless number of ways, and this fact is daunting for people looking not only for *any* way but also for a pattern of presentation that is known to be effective. Here are four basic, tried-and-true patterns. Their acceptance doesn't make them dull or predictable; those adjectives can only apply to your attitude, material, and delivery. Like outlines, patterns are blank slates, and are as powerful—or as bland—as you make them.

1. *Sequential.* Present events in the sequence they occur, e.g., the steps necessary to start a new business or to install a new computer. A *chronological* sequence goes further and gives a specific time context to the event. It's inherently logical and easy for an audience to follow.

2. *Categorical.* This pattern is useful when you lack a clear pattern of organization, or your topic isn't confined to a procedure, process, or time frame.

You assign meaningful labels to subtopics related to a general topic. For example, I deliver a speech on the topic "Sales Success" and within the speech I have four categories: "Personal Power," "Organizational Power," "Verbal Power," and "Sales Power." The categorical pattern works well when you are presenting new ideas that have not yet been put into a framework by your audience.

3. *Problem and solution.* This pattern is commonly used in technical presentations, but it is effective for any talk where you need to show what *is*, what *ought to be*, and what *needs to be done*. When you think about it, most good presentations state a problem. Either the problem itself or the consequences of not correcting it is the attention-getter. Often this pattern includes:

Symptoms of the problem. Get the audience to recognize that the problem exists and should be solved.

Identification of the "real" problem. Analyze and present the what, when, where, how much, how many, how often, and why. Show how the answers to these questions are related and state (or restate) objectives related to the problem.

Possible solutions. A talk addressing a problem of any complexity will not only list solutions but also include constraints on the solutions, an overall evaluation of them, and a recommendation of the best solution or combination of solutions.

You can use the problem-and-solution pattern most persuasively and dramatically when you want the audience to make a decision and take action. It's also very effective for presenting your findings in a dramatic context.

4. *Contrast and comparison.* Get your audience to evaluate alternative ideas or plans by calling its attention to differences and similarities. The success of managers with a closed mind versus those who are more flexible; "intrapreneuring" versus hiring outside consultants; the different ways two companies face a crisis—all use comparisons not only to illustrate but also to structure the argument.

Combinations: A Final Alternative

The four basic patterns can easily combine with each other. However you present your information, your task is to develop the optimal combination in terms of your topic, your audience, and your objectives of informing and persuading.

Each pattern can also benefit from a *question approach*,

where you stimulate the audience by rephrasing the point you're making as a question.

Before You Speak: Test Your Organization

You've focused, researched, outlined, written, polished, and you're ready to speak. Check your preparation against the following list of key characteristics of a well-organized speech:

- A clear purpose.
- A topic inherently interesting to the audience.
- Strong, logical, and clear sequence of ideas.
- Points presented in a consistent way that is easy to follow.
- Speech is adapted to the attitude of the audience and to any special circumstances.
- Transitions are clear, definite, and well thought out.
- There isn't too much information, and what is there relates directly to your main points.
- Plenty of support backs up your assertions.
- Frequent summaries aid the audience and emphasize your main points.
- The conclusion restates what it is you want your audience to know, do, or feel.

Once you have an outline you're comfortable with, it will be tempting to fill it in with as much information as possible to support your points. Avoiding that temptation is central to avoiding the next speaking fault, "too much information."

Professional Projects: Organizing Helps

Define your purpose and select the most appropriate pattern of organization.

1. You are a project manager in a large management consulting firm. You have been asked to give a presentation to a potential client on the benefits of using your company. Your purpose is to get a commitment from the client to use your company.
2. You must make a presentation to your staff on the importance of teamwork.
   Develop your organization through these two methods:
   A. Comparison and contrast
   B. Problem and solution

6

Fault #3:

Too Much Information

No speech can be entirely bad, if it is short enough.
　　　　　　　　　　　　　　　　　　—Irving S. Cobb

Faced with an expectant audience, speakers feel they have to provide as much detailed information as they can. This overabundance of information makes some speakers feel secure, and soon becomes their security blanket.

This love of information is understandable; as a country, we have been programmed toward overabundance—more is best. Not so with speeches. Although your speech should be rich in examples and illustrations, it should be thin in facts, figures, and lists. This is especially true for technical presentations, which tend to be overloaded with information.

Watch Out for the Multiplying Facts

Facts are seemingly reassuring. They back our assertions and give us ground to stand on. Worried speakers gather them for many reasons, not realizing an abundance is harmful to a speech, since it's a lot easier to compile data than to make them interesting. Some speakers use facts to back up their claims, thinking that the more information the audience gets, the more believable and compelling the speech will be. They use facts to give speeches an objective—and therefore powerful—tone. Other speakers feel the audience needs to know a lot and pile facts and lists into a speech in an attempt to give people their "money's worth."

However well intentioned, both approaches are misguided and work against both the speaker and the audience. Audience overload occurs surprisingly quickly. People retain three or four main points—nicely illustrated and explained—better than they do myriad bits of supporting information. Instead of bolstering your audience, excess facts just bog the audience down.

But the fact problem goes even deeper. An abundance of data is not the best support for your argument. Anyone can read a list of facts; your job is to make that information interesting, to give your viewpoint, using your own style and voice. Audiences don't want sheer objectivity: They want your interpretation.

Don't Dodge the Spotlight

Remember that you have been invited to speak for reasons that have nothing to do with your research abilities. You have something unique to say on the subject, some special angle.

My first job was teaching very bright high-school kids. I was a nervous wreck, because I figured that they were so much smarter than I was, which was undoubtedly true. I studied and studied before each class and ran a losing battle trying to stay ahead of them.

At the time, I didn't realize that I knew enough about the subject; I already had enough information. What I needed to do was believe I could make that information interesting and meaningful to the members of my audience. They may have had more intelligence, but I had the experience to translate the facts vividly. Once I realized they were there to hear my interpretation of the subject, I was fine.

Don't Let Data Equal Boredom

Even speeches that don't overload on information can be accused of having too much—if that information isn't interpreted in an interesting way. Granted, it's a lot easier to give information than to look for ways to make it interesting and useful. (But no one ever said giving a speech was easy.)

The major fault in technical presentations is relying on the hard-core technical data to carry the day, and having too much of it. Everyone—scientists included—wants a presentation that doesn't throw findings at him but interprets facts and weaves a story. Almost all of the technical presentations I have seen needed their information reduced by half and their visual aids simplified.

Humanize your data: After my son took a college course on military history, I asked him what struck him as the most interesting thing he had learned. He said he was amazed by how long it took soldiers to load the early guns and how difficult they were to fire. He saw the data presented to him in terms of human consequences. Let your audiences do the same by presenting your facts in a human context.

It's also very easy to make false assumptions about the level of data appropriate for your audience. For example, in talks to upper management, speakers feel they can fill speeches with technical information, since the audience is at so high a level. In fact, by the time people get to upper management, the skills they wield are generalists' skills; they are no longer as knowledgeable of the technical details as the technicians below them.

Power Through Condensation

If you embroider your facts with the stories and support that will make them memorable, chances are you will have too much to say. Condensing a speech you've worked hard on into the allotted time may seem cruel, unusual, and impossible. But it's necessary. When you take time to condense your speech, your audience is much more likely to listen to what you say, since longwindedness leads to repetition and lack of focus.

It takes time and thought to condense everything you know about a subject into a few highly refined major points. Woodrow Wilson, the last president to write his own speeches, was once asked how long it took him to prepare a ten-minute speech. "Two weeks," he said. And how long for an hour's talk? "One week." And for a two-hour presentation? "Oh," he said, "I'm ready now."

Some Rules to Speak By

In my speech classes, I give what seems like a simple assignment: Prepare a three-minute speech on any topic that interests you. That's only enough time for about 450 words. When these speeches are delivered, almost no one finishes in the allotted time. Some are only halfway through, some have five more slides to show, and some are still in the midst of their opening.

The problem is that most people have a very unrealistic idea of what they can say in a short period of time. And if people overload three minutes to such an extent, imagine what they will do with a twenty-minute speech! Everyone tries to fit in too much or tries to talk faster, as they realize they are running out of time. This time trap points out a key to a powerful speech or presentation: Practice—and time—your delivery. Even though the only way to really see if your speech fits a time limit is to practice it, here are some guidelines for length you can use *before* you write: If your speech should be twenty minutes, figure on covering four major points; thirty minutes leaves you room for five or six points; and a one-hour speech allows you to work in eight major points.

These limits make it sound like you don't have a lot of time and room—and you don't. It's staying power that you're after, and that means limiting yourself and choosing your main points with care. In each case, your points should be nicely illustrated, well explained, and tied together smoothly.

Respect Your Audience's Limits

An audience reaches its limit a lot faster and sooner than most speakers think. The average attention span is only eight seconds. People forget 25 percent of what they hear within twenty-four hours; 50 percent within forty-eight hours, and 80 percent in four days. Your words of wisdom will be competing with people's thoughts of what they did that day, what assignment is due tomorrow, and whether anyone's home to walk the dog. Being brief and concise isn't just polite, it's effective. And it helps you avoid the speaker's ultimate curse: being boring.

Think of the clergy, for example, Norman Vincent Peale or Robert Schuller—how clear they are; how few their main points; how clearly they explain those points. When you realize that a good speech is heavily weighted toward explanations and illustrations and not facts, you'll be well on your way to powerful presentations and ready to choose the right support to back up your ideas.

Professional Projects: Practice Editing

1. Select an article or editorial from your local paper. Condense it into one short paragraph. Be sure to get across the main point.
2. Take out your last twenty-minute presentation. Imagine you are the last speaker of the day and have only three minutes to deliver it. Jot down the key points you will make and what you can eliminate.

7

Fault #4: Not Enough Support

for Your Ideas, Concepts,

and Information

"I'm glad I attended your lecture on insomnia, doctor."
"Good. Did you find it interesting?"
"Not especially, but it did cure me of my insomnia!"
—Old Joke from a Humor Anthology

Interesting, memorable, powerful, and never boring—
that's a description any speaker would hope applies to his
or her speech. And the surest route to that kind of speaking success is using support—examples, anecdotes, and
other devices—throughout your talk. The PEP formula
(Point, Example, Point) is designed to let you weave in
examples and illustrations. Every major point you make
needs to be supported to be memorable.

Without support for your facts, audiences lose involvement in what you are saying. Many speakers work to make
their introduction and conclusions memorable but neglect
doing the same for the body of the speech. That's understandable: It's hard to sustain an audience's involvement
as you make every point. Although it may be hard, it's
also essential for powerful talks. Using examples to make
your talk lively is the best way to maintain that involvement. Examples with vivid language, colorful stories, and
famous sources wake up the audience and earn their attention.

Choose Your Stories with Care

Like any powerful tool, support can be overused and mis-
used. The PEP formula ensures that your speech doesn't
become a string of stories; support devices should bolster
your main points, not vice versa.

Make sure your supporting examples and quotes are well
rehearsed, accurate, and tie into your purpose. It's tempting to plunge ahead with a lively story or fact without
checking it thoroughly; after all, no one is going to write
down every word you say, and you are just trying to keep
people interested. But in any field or endeavor, mistakes
can come back to haunt you. The best speakers use accurate data, accepted definitions, and good sources. Finding authorities on your subject may take a little extra
research, but it's worth it.

Selling Through Stories

Speakers are in the selling business, and they sell facts by
using examples the audience is far more likely to retain
than straight facts. Use your support to *focus:* All of your
stories, jokes, analogies, and quotations must be related
to your subject.

It's very important to get into the habit of looking for
good stories that will make your speeches interesting. Audiences love people stories. During one PowerSpeak program, I asked people to tell a story about their first driving
test, first day at college, or first date—in twenty-five words
or less. I got a wonderful variety of interesting stories,
and afterward people said that was the best part of the
program, because it made them realize—vividly—the importance of stories.

Technical speakers must make sure they present a vivid
illustration or demonstration of their process, procedure,
or discovery. By doing so, they "translate" the esoteric
into the relevant. Developing this kind of support isn't just

more fun for your audience; it's more fun for you, too. It also shows the audience that you are comfortable with your topic and your expertise and that you care about giving the audience an enjoyable speech.

Support Is Everywhere

The best way to use support is to mix humor, quotations, analogies, and other elements—offer your audience a rich brew of stories. Mix human-interest stories with factual details and vice versa. Your sources? Try newspapers, quotation collections, industry research, memories of childhood, friends' experiences, world history, and so on. Your sources are endless. And never underestimate the power of the past. I often use the following quotation from Confucius to open sessions where I'm speaking on effective management (I came upon it one night in a Chinese restaurant, in the middle of a very big fortune cookie):

> First, putting a man to death without having taught him what is right—that is called savagery. Second, to expect a task to be completed at a certain date without having given the worker warning—that is oppression. Third, to be vague in the orders you give while expecting absolute punctiliousness—that is being a tormentor. Finally, to give someone his due in a grudging way— that is contemptible and petty.

This quotation never fails to bring nods of recognition, and looks of surprise, when people hear that Confucius came up with this wisdom around 500 B.C.! Reminding people that there's nothing new under the sun and giving your presentation a historical context are good ways to make your speech something people can relate to and remember.

Tried-and-True Sources of Support

Whether you're facing a skeptical audience, have a difficult idea to communicate, or just need support to make your topic clear and engaging, here are some of the most reliable ways to give your speech staying power. You'll keep your audience involved and its interest level high if every three or four minutes during your presentation, you tell a story, ask a question, or use a combination of the support devices that follow:

■ *Facts.* A fact is simply a statement that can be verified, either by referring to a third source or by direct observation. Facts give your opinions weight and add objectivity to your pronouncements. Without facts, you have no credibility. The key is not to bore your audience with too many of them.

■ *Figures and statistics.* Succinct, unblinking—numbers can provide startling punctuation to any presentation and are mandatory in many technical ones. But numbers cannot communicate on their own. Some numbers are so vast they require further illustration, like the national deficit. A good speaker will "translate" this huge sum into a stack of $100 bills and tell the audience how tall that stack is.

■ *Definitions.* They allow you to inquire into the nature of something, usually by identifying it with a general class and then specifying its particular qualities. For example, a man (the word to be defined) is a type of mammal (general class) that walks upright (particular quality).

Using the dictionary is always a good source, though definitions can vary. Select the definition that suits you. For instance, if you want to call attention to marketing's sheer scope, you can define it as "the coordination of all activities—including planning, research, and selling—necessary to get a product or service from a seller to a buyer."

Definitions don't have to be serious; many speakers use

pithy, witty quotations to zero in on a point they want to cover. Here's how Ambrose Bierce defined "egotist": "A person more interested in himself than in me."

■ *Examples.* Usually brief, examples are incidents or objects that prove or clarify a generalization you're making. As support, examples are everywhere and often serve to introduce compelling facts and statistics. A manager trying to prove it's possible to cut costs in his division without cutting personnel will persuade his audience with examples: the actual dollar savings attached to various changes in procedure.

While you will usually want to use examples to prove or elaborate on your point, you can also use them to form a positive point of view—e.g., as XYZ Manufacturing Company has shown, if you don't cut personnel, here's what will result: Morale will rise, employees will work harder, and profits will increase.

■ *Illustrations.* These are more detailed than examples, often offering point-by-point clarification.

To illustrate the above stance on not cutting personnel, you could go step by step and show how the company was still able to cut costs through a better hiring process, and then take your listeners through that process.

■ *Anecdotes and personal stories.* These are stories or experiences used to illuminate but not necessarily to prove a point. Many speakers use anecdotes and personal stories—often about themselves—to establish rapport, break the ice, or subtly reinforce the point they are making. Anecdotes tend to be human-interest stories and can have real staying power with an audience.

Here's one I used during a talk on leadership: I wanted to get across the idea that leadership is something you have to earn. My husband and I were playing tennis, not serving formally, but just hitting the ball around. A kid watching this competition asked if he could be our ball boy. Naturally, we were thrilled, since we had never had the privilege before. I noticed he kept returning the balls to my husband, even though he wasn't hitting better shots, he seemed to have control of the game. I wanted those balls returned to me. So I concentrated hard, hit three winners my husband returned right into the net, and was rewarded with the kid sending balls my way—exclusively. It was clear I had earned the right to serve—not by anything I said, but by my actions.

■ *Authority.* Cite an authority when you use a reliable, recognized source to support your point.

■ *Quotations.* A favorite of many speakers, quotations allow you to bring in an authority, an example, and often some humor—all at once. And since many quotations that have survived through the ages tend to be pithy and profound, speakers instantly inject both qualities into their speech.

■ *Testimony.* Usually more directly relevant to the speaker's points than a quotation, testimony is corroborating evidence—proof in someone else's words that supports your view.

■ *Analogies.* A set of parallel conditions that throw light on what is being discussed by their similarity and familiarity. Analogies are very useful in technical presentations. Use a "domestic" analogy, one that defines the esoteric in terms that are close to home. Saying the power lines of New York City are like a vast spiderweb brings a vivid image to mind. Best-selling author Dr. Richard Selzer makes medicine seem immediate when he writes phrases like "a surgeon, who palms the human heart as though it were some captured bird." The best analogies have a little bit of surprise—the surprise that leads to retention.

■ *Restatements.* Since it is the business of a good speaker to condense and edit, restatements help you find and present the essence in a long-winded point you need to include. By putting things into your own words, which is why you were asked to speak in the first place, restatements let you speak with the authority of the facts behind the statement without losing your own talent.

■ *Historical background.* Most presentations need some

sort of context to be persuasive. Be sure your audience has the background necessary to understand the implications of your presentation. Don't make the mistake of assuming the topic you're talking about is common knowledge. Astute speakers will present their background material in such a way that it also supports their contentions.

Keep Your Flourishes Coming

Speakers also get support from devices such as humor, rhetorical questions, and compliments or challenges directed toward the audience. Whether used separately or as part of an example, an analogy, or another element, these attention-getters serve to startle; they make the audience sit up and take notice, and they allow you to observe the cardinal rule of speaking: Never be boring.

A good speaker will insert some lively support every three to four minutes to keep audience involvement high and to recapture attention. A speech should be made up of a series of peaks and valleys: The peaks are the places where the speaker inserts supporting material; the valleys are the natural lows between new bits of material that make the peaks possible.

Most speakers start strong, then plummet as they move toward the conclusion, where the excitement builds and the final point is made. But chances are that what came in the middle will be lost.

The most effective speech travels an interesting path, guiding the audience along through each section with introductions, transitions, and conclusions. Supporting material will be frequent but not so overpacked that it slows down the journey. Momentum is steady and sure, climbing up to a memorable conclusion.

The world is filled with support for your presentations. Look around, keep lists of things that strike you as appropriate, and remember to use examples to make your points effectively. Carry around a little black book to jot down support as it occurs to you. Make it an ongoing quest; you should always be looking for examples.

When we tell stories, our voices naturally become animated. Once you have amassed your support, the next step is to really use your voice, raising and lowering it for variety. Your voice is an instrument you can use to keep your audience interested, an advantage the next chapter covers in detail.

Professional Projects: Build Interest and Involvement

1. You have been asked to deliver an orientation address to twenty new employees. In your opening include at least one analogy and one personal story.
2. Start a file for quotations, stories, and all kinds of supporting materials.

8

Fault #5: Monotonous

Voice and Sloppy Speech

Speech is a mirror of the soul. As a man speaks so he is.
—Publius Syrus

Your voice is your calling card. Over the phone, it's responsible for the entire impression you make on your listener. Whether you bore or enthrall—a lot depends on how you sound.

People's initial perceptions of each other break down three ways: visually (how we appear), vocally (how we sound), and verbally (what we say). Yet the verbal aspect accounts for only 7 percent of how we are perceived; how we look forms 55 percent of the impression, and how we sound a surprising 38 percent. Yet the sound of our voice is something we give little thought to.

But you have to be conscious of your voice—and of how to change it—throughout your speech. As anyone who has heard a droning speaker knows, the wrong voice, besides making a bad impression, wrecks an otherwise compelling speech. A monotonous tone, mumbling, lack of clarity, and poor enunciation leave the audience noticing your voice and not your words.

A voice is not a neutral thing: It's either a wonderful asset or a serious liability. It either conveys control and confidence or proves a lack of both. But it should be your *greatest aid* in being interesting and exciting, because it can insert variety into a speech with such ease. To battle an audience's short attention span, speakers need to insert something interesting every three to four minutes. But that doesn't mean coming up with stories and jokes exclusively; you can use your voice to get attention immediately. You can polish your voice just as you polish your speech. All it takes is awareness and practice.

Listen to Yourself—Often

The first step to a powerful voice is getting to know yours. That's not as silly as it sounds. You may think you know your voice; after all, you're always speaking to people at work, at home, and on the phone. But in those instances you're listening to *them*, not to yourself.

Getting your voice ready for a speech means listening to the way you start sentences, form vowels, and pause after periods. You should practice speaking aloud often. Use your own words, the newspaper, anything. Read to the kids, to the dog; recite in the shower. Develop a love for good speech; listen to audiocassettes of powerful speakers reading book excerpts. Listen to how classically trained actors like Laurence Olivier or Meryl Streep use their voices, as instruments of feeling.

Look in the mirror to see how you are making the sounds. Make a habit of speaking aloud to yourself every day. Use a tape recorder and the exercises in this chapter and *listen* to your progress. Evaluate yourself often; use the form at the end of this chapter. Once you have started to listen to your voice objectively, you're ready to tackle the fine points of controlling it.

How to Get More Vocal Variety

Speakers have many tools at their disposal for making their voice interesting:

- *Volume*. Volume adds variety to whatever you say. Practice: Say the word *no* over and over, starting very softly (almost whispering) and working your way to very loud (almost shouting).

■ *Pitch and inflection.* Different from volume, pitch and inflection reflect your overall tone.

Practice: Say the following, letting your voice follow the words: "Let your voice come down evenly, smoothly as a sigh. Then evenly up and ever so high. Hold our tones level and high today; then level and low tomorrow, I say. Let tones glide high, then slide down low. Learn to say no, no, NO." Recite the "do, re, mi" scale, going from a high tone to a low one. Or try the numbers one through eight, going up the scale and coming down again.

■ *Pace and rhythm.* How fast or slow you articulate the words and sounds.

Practice: Enjoy this old rhyme. Slow down each time you say "Broom, green Broom" and the words that rhyme with it. Read the rest very quickly.

There was an old man lived out in the wood
Whose trade was cutting of Broom, green Broom!
He had but one son without thrift, without good,
Who lay in his bed 'til 'twas noon, bright noon.

The old man awoke one morning and spoke,
He swore he would fire the room, that room,
If his John would not rise and open his eyes,
And away to the wood to cut Broom, green Broom.

So Johnny arose, and he slipped on his clothes,
And away to the wood to cut Broom, green Broom;
He sharpened his knives, and for once he contrives
To cut a bundle of Broom, green Broom.

When Johnny passed under a fine lady's house,
Passed under a lady's fine room, fine room
She called to her maid, "Go fetch to my side,
Go fetch to my side the boy that sells Broom, green
  Broom."

When Johnny came into that fine lady's house
And stood in that lady's fine room;
"Young Johnny my lad, will you give up your trade,
And marry a lady in bloom, full bloom?"

John gave his consent and to church they both went
And he married the lady in bloom, full bloom.
At Market and fair all the folks do declare
There's none like the boy that sold Broom, green Broom.*

■ *Emphasis.* This affects your word and syllable stress. The key point is to be sure people get your main ideas. Help them by subverting the less important ones. A common fault of speakers is to emphasize too many things; you should isolate the key points you want to emphasize.

Practice: Use a simple declarative statement such as "I am going to the store." Use the same sentence to answer a series of questions, emphasizing the appropriate word to answer the question. Subvert the unimportant words.

Who is going to the store: *I* am going to the store.
Are you coming from or going to the store? I am *going to* the store.
Where are you going? To the bakery? I am going to the *store.*

■ *Attitude.* The same word or phrase can take on radically different meanings, depending on the attitude implicit in your voice.

Practice: Say *well* as if you were:

Annoyed
Disgusted
Surprised
Thrilled

*"Green Broom" reprinted with permission of editors Lilene Mansell and Timothy Monich from Edith Warman Skinner's *Speak with Distinction* (New Brunswick, N.J., publisher unknown, 1965), p. 19.

In doubt
Suspicious
Thoughtful
Pugnacious

■ *The pause.* Powerful speakers use the pause several ways—for emphasis, effect, and mood. Pauses can be long, medium, short, or very short—when you're just drawing a breath. They can also signal a transition.

Practice: The next time you have to deliver good news, practice your pause. "Wait until I tell you the good news!" Stop. Count to three slowly. You'll sense the anticipation in your listeners. Enjoy it and feel its power. Then tell them the news.

Learn to Loosen Up

Tense people have more monotonous voices, because they are not using their jaws and not changing their tone enough. An effective voice is relaxed and flexible; the variety so important to a lively speech will only result if you have loosened up your voice ahead of time and speak with an open throat and a loose, active lower jaw. With an open throat, sounds are no longer tight and squeezed.

To open your throat, relax the whole area around it: Rotate your head slowly to one side for a count of eight, and repeat for the other side. Think of clothes dangling on a line—limp and at ease. Then indulge in a nice big yawn. Right before you finish the yawn, lazily recite the vowels—"A,E,I,O,U." All your throat exercises should be put together with very open sounds and done very lazily, effortlessly, and slowly.

Now work on getting an active jaw. Americans are known to have tight jaws, which makes for poor diction. You have to open up your jaw on certain vowel sounds and diphthongs (vowel sounds that come together, like *now*).

Say *cow,* with your hand on your jaw, and notice the jaw movement.

Practice: Try "How now, brown cow." Make these sounds slowly and easily. Use a mirror to make sure you are really shaping the sounds. The tight jaw style of Gary Cooper and Clint Eastwood may be great for movies, but it's not good for public speakers.

More Loosening Exercises.

Throat. Rotate your head, get relaxed. Drop your lower jaw as if you were about to yawn and say: you, you, you, you. Then try:

> With a yeo-heave-ho, for the wind is free,
> Her anchor's a-trip and her helm's a-lee,
> Hurrah for the homeward bound!
> Yeo-ho-heave-ho,
> Hurrah for the homeward bound.*

Lips. To loosen your lips, say:

P	P	P	P
PP	PP	PP	PP
PPP	PPP	PPP	PPP
PPPP	PPPP	PPPP	PPPP

Tongue. To get your tongue flexible, try:

> Mrs. Peck Pigeon
> Is picking for bread
> Bob-bob-bob
> Goes her little round head.
> Tame as a pussy-cat

*From Gilbert and Sullivan's *The Mikado* reprinted with permission of the editors Lilene Mansell and Timothy Monich from Edith Warman Skinner's *Speak with Distinction* (New Brunswick, N.J., publisher unknown, 1965), p. 9.

In the street
Step-step-step
Go her little red feet.
With her little red feet
And her little round head,
Mrs. Peck-Pigeon
Goes picking for bread.*

Other Keys to Clear Diction

Our breathing, throats, and jaws all play an important role in how we sound. But clear diction is also governed by our lips, teeth, and tongue. Lips should hit against each other on the "P", "B", "N", "W," and "WH" sounds.

Practice: Create these sounds and the vowels in between by saying "PAPA," "MAMA," and "WAWA." Make sure your lips hit each other and build your speed. Try longer phrases, increasing your speed as you go along: "We have rubber baby buggy bumpers." "Peter Prangle picked pickly prangly pears."

Keep practicing until you have an open throat, an active lower jaw, strong lip muscles, and a flexible tongue that can trip lightly over tongue twisters.

Peter Piper pick'd a Peck of Pickled Peppers:
Did Peter Piper pick a Peck of Pickled Peppers?
If Peter Piper pick'd a peck of Pickled Peppers,
Where's the Peck of Pickled Peppers Peter Piper pick'd?†

A tooter who tooted a flute
   Tried to tutor two tutors to toot.
   Said the two to their tutor,

---

*Reprinted with permission of editors Lilene Mansell and Timothy Monich from Edith Warman Skinner's *Speak with Distinction* (New Brunswick, N.J., publisher unknown, 1965), p. 15.
†Reprinted from Leroy Phillips' *Peter Piper's Practical Principles of Plain and Perfect Pronunciation.* New York: Dover Publications, 1970.

"Is it harder to toot or
To tutor two tutors to toot?"*

Achieve Variety Through Emphasis

Vocal variety is one of the most powerful weapons in a speaker's arsenal; good speakers use it to great effect. If your words were written, you would rely on punctuation to move your thoughts along and to link your ideas. In speech, all you have to make your points and to get people to understand is your voice; it is the only sort of punctuation the speaker has.

An effective speaker stresses points by limiting the main ones and by shading all the rest through vocal technique. The key words you emphasize, the pauses you insert, your shifting pitch, rhythm, loudness, tone, and rate of speech all affect how your audience interprets your words. Learn to *build;* even lists can gain drama if you let your voice add it. For example, "I came, I saw, I conquered" could be said with equal emphasis on the three verbs, and it would seem rather bland. But "I came, I saw, (pause) I *conquered*" builds to a finale and catches the audience's attention.

You should always "lean" on the new idea in your sentence. For example, if you've been mentioning sales success and are introducing the concept of life success, emphasize the word *life* vocally, since it represents a new idea, and de-emphasize success, since you've said it already. Nine times out of ten an action word (often a verb) represents the new idea; don't leave it entirely up to the audience to grasp the new idea just because it's new; use your voice to nudge the audience along.

Another way to highlight an important point is to stop

*Used by permission of Sterling Publishing Co., Inc., from *The Biggest Tongue Twister Book in the World,* by Gyles Brandreth, © 1978 by Sterling Publishing Co., Inc., Two Park Avenue, New York, NY 10016.

talking just before you introduce the point. The pause is one of the most effective attention-getters around. People get so used to hearing a speaker *talk* that when there is silence they sit up and take notice. In fact, a long pause is an excellent way to begin a talk: You've been introduced; you're at the podium looking out at the audience . . . a pause now gets everyone's attention, since people don't know when or how you are going to begin. Result? You appear firmly in control.

Keep Your Speech Interesting Through Articulation, Diction, and Pronunciation

When you speak, you avail yourself of words the way a musician uses notes. And like the musician, you can sound words and letters smoothly or disconcertingly. All it takes to be smooth is some awareness of language. The way we speak breaks down into three elements:

1. Articulation means using your articulators—lips, tongue, teeth, lower jaw, upper gums, hard and soft palate, and throat—to form the sounds of speech. The key to good articulation is keeping all these parts flexible as you speak.
2. Diction is the total production of your sounds. You can be sloppy or crisp, depending on how you put everything together.
3. Pronunciation is the manner in which you deliver words; it's where you place your accent. People in different regions pronounce differently; *car* in New York becomes *cah* in Boston. Some people say *e*laborate instead of e*lab*orate. You have to be careful: I once heard a Russian woman deliver an address on the subject of nuclear power at a public utility. When she said *mass* (frequently), it sounded to those in the audience like *mess* and they were noticeably alarmed and confused.

The clearer your articulation, diction, and pronunciation are, the more in control—and the more powerful—you will appear to be.

Don't Ignore the Basics—Vowels and Consonants

Vowels are the music of our speech; they carry the tone and must be pronounced like the open and pure letters they are. *Consonants* are the bones of speech; they must be sharp and precise. *Diphthongs* are a union of two vowels that form one syllable, but that one syllable must be formed properly.

When forming all vowels, the tip of your tongue should be behind your lower teeth. The two major problems people have with vowels are elongating the short ones and not drawing out the long ones. Keep your jaw active and your tongue flexible and you will avoid these mistakes.

Practice: Explore the differences between "He bit the dust," where the vowels are short and clipped, and "the long sleeve," where the sounds should be drawn out.

Reading out loud is still the best way to become aware of the various sounds speakers face. Inside our small, twenty-six-letter alphabet lurk a surprising variety of combinations. We have only five vowels, but fourteen vowel sounds are possible. Our nineteen consonants can produce twenty-five consonant sounds—like the "dg" in *udge*. The more aware you are of these components, the more practiced you are at uttering them, the more polished you will sound.

Vowel, Diphthong, and Consonant Exercises

Sentences for Practicing Vowels

ē   Where secret seas of eager blue beat on coralline reefs.

i   Philip limited his civilian activities.

e	Tell Betty Fred says it was an excellent effort.
a	The man from Annapolis had cash guaranteed.
ü	Who will cool the fruit juice with two soup spoons?
ủ	He pulled and shook and cooked the good book.
ō	Olivia evoked a vociferous ovation.
ȯ	I saw all the daughters fall on the broad lawn.
ä	Popular John's watch shop was near the political offices.
ɑ:	Father parked the car and was tardy to the large party.
ɜ:	The nervous girl murmured at the first rehearsal.
a	The actor had bad acne.
ə	The American actor accomplished the difficult task.
ʌ:	The humble judge refunded the money.

Sentences for Practicing Diphthongs

ā	Waken lords and ladies gay.
ī	Surprise the child with the ice cream pie.
oi	The joyful noise employed our voices.
ō	He'll go alone and bring home some coal.
aủ	The howling hounds went round and round our house.
iə	The auctioneer volunteered a chandelier with real veneer.
aə	Beware the precarious stairway.
ủə	While touring, the people had to endure a detour.
ōə	I adore the shore as of yore.

Sentences for Practicing Consonants

'p	The previous principal promised the primary pupils promotions.
'b	A blue-blooded beggar saw a beautiful suburban bungalow.
'm	I remember my mother and dream of home.
hw	Why whine when reading Whistler and Whitman?
'w	The wise woman wore warm woolens.

*:=phonetic symbol used to represent sound.

f	Familiar friends offered fudge and fruit.
v	Wave upon wave of active reservists made a decisive victory.
'th	Truth thrives through thick and thin.
<u>th</u>	They bother those that hear them.
't	Lady Teazle teases and tantalizes Sir Peter.
'd	This I beheld or dreamed it in a dream.
'n	Nancy Noonan the nun needs no nonsense especially when running and sunning.
'l	Little leaves lie on the lovely lake.
's	Sidney sits by six sick city slickers.
'z	Suzanna Zorro loves her red zinger tea.
sh	She shot the associate and shrieked her confession.
zh	The treasurer had a vision of a pleasurable treasure hunt.
r	Through an error they served carrots, radishes, currants, and raspberries.
'y	The Yale graduate yearned to tutor at the institute.
'k	The questionable choir quarreled over the frequently quoted quality of the quartet.
g	The gorgeous girl giggled at his gruff dialogue.
ŋ	The singer sang a long song swelling and sweeping.
h	Helen with her head held high heard the highway horns from their home on the high hill.
ch	The butcher chose a chunk of chopped chuck.
j	I was obliged to discharge the beseiged jury.

Breathe Correctly

For your audience to hear you, you must breathe correctly. People tend to start sentences on a high note and fade out; their voices start to sound monotonous because they don't have enough breath to support variety throughout the entire sentence. A good voice has sufficient breath so that the audience hears all the important sounds.

We get into bad habits and don't use our breathing fully. To really see how to breathe, watch babies or animals. To breathe fully, like they do, take a deep breath and observe yourself. Did you use only your shoulders and chest or did your diaphragm expand, too? (That's the area just above your waist.) As you inhale, your diaphragm should expand, and it should deflate like a balloon as you exhale.

Find Your Diaphragm

To get your diaphragm going, pant like a dog out of breath. Put your hand above your waist. Now, laugh—when you laugh you are actually breathing through your diaphragm. It's like a large band all around this area of your body. To exercise your diaphragm, lie down with an object like a heavy book pressing against your chest.

Practice: Raise the book up and down and get used to breathing through your diaphragm. When you're standing, practice not lifting your shoulders as you breathe: Proper breathing isn't seen or heard by your audience.

It's not just how you take in air, but how much. If you take in too much you are going to flood your diaphragm; if you take in too little, your voice will sound very thin. You have to learn to distribute air evenly over an entire sentence, and it's a good idea to take in a little extra so you don't run out of steam. Since the most important point usually comes at the end of a sentence, you'll want to have enough energy to really make your point there.

Get into the habit of taking air in through your nose and letting it out through your mouth; this way your mouth doesn't get dry, which is a common speaking fear. Speaking through your mouth will only accentuate whatever dryness is already there.

Build Your Endurance

Short phrases only require short breaths. But complex sentences pose challenges for speakers, who don't want to weaken points by stopping in the middle and gasping—

however slightly—for air. You can control your need for air just as people train themselves to stay underwater for long periods.

Start by saying a short sentence first. Then add phrases one at a time while extending your endurance.

Practice: "This is the cow, with the crumpled horn, that tossed the dog, that worried the cat, that killed the rat, that ate the food, that lay in the house that Jack built." You can also use "The Twelve Days of Christmas."

The first day of Christmas my true love sent
   to me a partridge in a pear tree.

The second day of Christmas my true love sent
   to me two turtle doves and a partridge in a
   pear tree.

The third day of Christmas my true love sent
   to me three French horns, two turtle doves
   and a partridge in a pear tree.

The fourth day of Christmas my true love
   sent to me four colly-birds, three
   French horns, two turtle doves and a
   partridge in a pear tree.

The fifth day of Christmas my true love
   sent to me five gold rings, four colly-
   birds, three French horns, two turtle
   doves and a partridge in a pear tree.

The sixth day of Christmas my true love sent
   to me six geese a-laying, five gold
   rings, four colly-birds, three French
   horns, two turtle doves and a partridge
   in a pear tree.

The seventh day of Christmas my true love
   sent to me seven swans a-swimming, six
   geese a-laying, five gold rings. Four
   colly-birds, three French horns, two

turtle doves and a partridge in a pear tree.

The eighth day of Christmas my true love sent to me eight maids a-milking, seven swans a-swimming, six geese a-laying, five gold rings. Four colly-birds, three French horns, two turtle doves and a partridge in a pear tree.

The ninth day of Christmas my true love sent to me nine drummers drumming, eight maids a-milking, seven swans a-swimming, six geese a-laying, five gold rings. Four colly-birds, three French horns, two turtle doves and a partridge in a pear tree.

The tenth day of Christmas my true love sent to me ten pipers piping, nine drummers drumming, eight maids a-milking, seven swans a-swimming, six geese a-laying, five gold rings. Four colly-birds, three French horns, two turtle doves and a partridge in a pear tree.

The eleventh day of Christmas my true love sent to me eleven ladies dancing, ten pipers piping, nine drummers drumming, eight maids a-milking, seven swans a-swimming, six geese a-laying, five gold rings. Four colly-birds, three French horns, two turtle doves and a partridge in a pear tree.

The twelfth day of Christmas my true love sent to me twelve lords a-leaping, eleven ladies dancing, ten pipers piping, nine drummers drumming, eight maids a-milking, seven swans a-swimming, six

geese a-laying, five gold rings. Four
colly-birds, three French horns, two
turtle doves and a partridge in a pear
tree.*

Each day you practice—and lengthen the sentence—your
endurance grows.

Your Path to a Powerful Voice

Although there are many voice pitfalls we can fall into
almost without knowing it, there are also many steps that
assure us of clear and effective communication:

- Use a warm, resonant voice. Avoid sounding flat, gruff,
  harsh, too weak, or too loud. Strive for a clear, ringing
  tone and speak with vigor.
- Build your point vocally. Add emphasis and drama
  through the way you actually say your words by stress-
  ing the most important words and phrases and shading
  the less important ones.
- Vary your pitch, force, volume, rate, and rhythm. Catch
  people's attention by getting noticeably louder at an
  important point.
- Have enough breath to finish each sentence on a strong
  note.
- Make sure your thoughts forge ahead and build your
  argument.
- Display a lively amount of vocal and physical energy.
  Be animated; otherwise, why should your audience be
  enthusiastic?
- Use rhetorical questions to involve your audience, but
  don't overdo it.

*"The Twelve Days of Christmas" reprinted with permission of editors
Lilene Mansell and Timothy Monich from Edith Warman Skinner's
Speak with Distinction (New Brunswick, N.J., publisher unknown,
1965), p. 98.

- Clearly articulate each sentence, phrase, word, and syllable. Give full value to all the sounds in your speech.
- Do not drop consonants (e.g., gonna, runnin').
- Use correct pronunciation.
- Strive for a smooth tone; it will sustain your argument better than a choppy one.
- Avoid "oh," "uh," "OK" and "you know."
- Make sufficient use of the pause.
- Make sure your voice rises when you ask questions and falls when you make statements.
- Use emphasis, pauses, inflections, changing pitch, and loudness to shade what you have to say.

A Quick Fix for Imminent Engagements

To guard against being boring, add variety to your next speech. Here is a quick list of things you can add without much trouble—things you *should* add to ensure that your next speech will be livelier than your last.

- Put at least two rhetorical questions in your speech. Your voice will naturally rise when you come to them.
- Insert at least one dramatic pause. This device builds your power, for nothing captures the audience's attention like silence.
- Vary your speed. If you tend to speak quickly, slow down at least three times during your presentation; if you speak slowly, speed up at least three times.
- Change your voice and your attitude just before your conclusion.
- Combine an interesting variety of voice inflections within your speech to involve your audience. The next chapter goes into meeting those needs in detail. Adding variety to your voice is important in general communication as well. Colleagues will listen more closely when you color your words to give emphasis to your important points.

Relax, You Probably Sound Fine

Speaking well is an art, not a science, and there is no one formula for a compelling voice. Whether you tend to speak fast or slow, you don't have to completely change the way you present words. Just become aware of the little things you can do to change the way you sound and practice the voice exercises in this chapter. Then at your next presentation, be natural and be yourself.

Professional Projects: Developing a More Interesting Voice

1. Develop a three- to five-minute vocal warm-up for yourself.
2. Record your next presentation or record a practice reading. Then evaluate it using the voice and speech evaluation form at the end of this chapter.
3. Use this evaluation form after every presentation to critique yourself.
4. Give this evaluation form to your boss or spouse while practicing your next presentation.

VOICE AND SPEECH EVALUATION FORM

1. *Voice production*

   a. Support of tone

      ___Good   ___Needs improvement   ___Weak

   b. Proper breathing

      ___Good   ___Needs improvement   ___Weak

   c. Vocal quality (e.g., harsh, nasal, breathy)

      ___Good   ___Needs improvement   ___Weak

   d. Resonance

      ___Good   ___Needs improvement   ___Weak

   e. Overall vocal energy

      ___Good   ___Needs improvement   ___Weak

2. *Producing the sounds*

   a. Sharp articulation

      ___Good   ___Needs improvement   ___Weak

   b. Flexible lips, jaw, tongue

      ___Good   ___Needs improvement   ___Weak

   c. Clear and correct pronunciation

      ___Good   ___Needs improvement   ___Weak

   d. Diction using long and short vowels

      ___Good   ___Needs improvement   ___Weak

3. *Vocal variety*

   a. Volume

___Good   ___Needs improvement   ___Weak

b. Pace or rhythm

___Good   ___Needs improvement   ___Weak

c. Pitch

___Good   ___Needs improvement   ___Weak

d. Inflection

___Good   ___Needs improvement   ___Weak

e. Attitude

___Good   ___Needs improvement   ___Weak

f. Shading and word emphasis

___Good   ___Needs improvement   ___Weak

g. Use of long and short forms

___Good   ___Needs improvement   ___Weak

h. Use of the pause

___Good   ___Needs improvement   ___Weak

4. *Main areas for improvement* _____

_____

_____

9

Fault #6: Not Meeting the

Real Needs of Your Audience

Men are not against you. They are merely for themselves.
—Gene Fowler

I once heard a woman at a conference give a speech on what new associations could do to grow, prosper, and be valuable to members. She had an audience that really cared about the topic; people had signed up for it specifically. She meandered, went off on tangents, and seldom finished a thought. She said "you know" about seventy-five times in a forty-five-minute presentation. But *because she met the needs of members of her audience,* she got a standing ovation. They felt she cared about them and understood what interested them. That's how important it is to be tuned in to your audience: If you are, even a poorly delivered speech can be well received; if you're not, even a polished one can fall flat.

A surprising number of speeches simply don't meet the real needs of the audience. The chief reason: The speaker feels it's enough to tell people something *the speaker* thinks they need to know. But you can't expect your audience to have the same excitement that you do; you must develop the audience's interest. No matter how worthy, life-enhancing, or even lifesaving your topic may be, your enthusiasm is not enough. You must make those in your audience enthusiastic. They are potential skeptics, and your task is to win them over. Since you can't say everything there is to say on your topic, you need to say the things your audience needs to hear.

The Most Compelling Subjects

Winning listeners over is easier if you know the four things people find most interesting: sex, health, money, and themselves. This is something of a cynic's list, but most good speeches will tap into one of the things, usually the last item.

Make It Impossible *Not* to Listen

Since people do things for their own reasons, you must motivate them from *their* perspectives, not yours. If you speak to their real needs, they will be compelled to listen, and listen well. In my own seminars and speeches, I always find out one or two specific problems that the audience currently faces. Then I construct a speech that solves—or shows people how to solve—those problems. This is the speaker as hero or heroine, the problem-solver approach, and I recommend it highly. If you're speaking to middle managers on running their departments more efficiently, and you determine that one of their problems is motivating clerical employees, then give them a strategy to do just that, with results that tie in to what the corporation expects of them.

Whether your audience is one person or one thousand, you should focus on its needs. Being successful in one-on-one situations requires you to focus on the other person. Start any general communication by putting yourself in that other person's shoes and proceed from there.

Addressing problems your audience faces illustrates the importance of *context*. So does this story: Suppose you came to a seminar and instead of the promised speaker you were met by a desert survival expert. You probably would not listen too closely. But if the pilot of a plane being forced to land in the desert gave that lecture, you would view that formerly irrelevant information quite differently. Context is caring—what does your audience care about? Figure that out, and you're well on your way.

Tune into WIIFM and Sell Benefits

Speakers should always be motivated by their desire to please the audience; audiences are motivated by their own self-interest. Both forms of self-interest come together well if you realize that every person you're talking to is thinking "Why should I care about this speech?" Everyone has a secret radio station called WIIFM, otherwise known as "What's In It For Me?" An effective speaker anticipates this built-in bias and shapes a speech by always thinking "What benefit or benefits can I offer this particular audience?"

You sell an audience with benefits, not facts. To use the old expression, you buy a drill not for the drill but for the hole. A ball-point pen has a retractable point (fact), so you don't get ink on you (benefit). But be careful of just throwing benefits at your audience; the connection between the product and the benefit—in this case the retractable point—must always be clear, because that's often the item or outlook you are trying to promote. Never assume that the members of the audience will make the connection themselves.

At first glance, this advice may sound cynical: People are so narrow-minded that everything must be fed to them in terms of self-interest. Not everything; just your speech. Think about it from this perspective: As a speaker, you are taking up people's time; you are asking them to listen closely to you for a period of time and to think hard about what you are saying. It may be cynical (and practical) to appeal to their needs, but it's also polite. They are giving you their time; you must respond with something worthy of that honor. In the end everyone benefits, especially you, since you will have succeeded in making your points in a vivid, convincing, and memorable fashion.

Seven Steps to Involving Your Audience

By addressing the needs of the people in your audience, you are *involving* them in your speech. The more you can make them participants and not passive listeners, the more effective you will be. By participants I don't mean people who bombard you during a question-and-answer session, but people who are thinking, reacting, and taking mental notes as you speak. Here are seven steps that help you instill the participation that leads to the persuasion that occurs when the audience follows your argument and actually accepts your ideas:

1. Prepare your speech with care, so your listeners will know you care about them and their needs.

2. Make the audience want to hear you; devise an intriguing, startling opening and a title you know will fit that audience.

3. Present your ideas dramatically, with stories, examples, and facts. You want people to remember what you say, and the support stories provide goes a long way toward making your speech vivid.

4. Show how those ideas affect the people in your audience and what the benefits are. They now have the facts—you've supplied them. Now bridge the gap between your words and their lives. If you want your department to make formal use of job descriptions when hiring, tell them why: how these documents will help them find qualified people, save time, work more efficiently with the personnel department, and so on.

5. Use language's most appealing words: discovery, easy, guaranteed, health, love, money, new, proven, results, safety, save, and you.

6. Draw them in; ask the listeners to study or contemplate these ideas further. Involve them. Show them your ideas have a relevant context; they aren't just your private, unsubstantiated thoughts.

7. Ask the audience to act on your ideas. The best speeches carry over—into petitions, changed minds, reorganizations, elections, new ways of doing things. Your end can be the point where you reveal that formerly hidden purpose that guided your speech from the beginning. But it was never meant to be kept a secret. By the end of your speech, you should have built the logic, the facts, and the stories to such a point that no one doubts your commitment. Now you are trying to enlist the troops.

Technical Presentation Pitfalls

I do a lot of consulting work with large corporations like Mobil Oil and Duke Power. More often than not, executives there who have to make presentations assume they can just give the facts, however technical, because their audience is technically inclined.

Don't make the same mistake; don't assume benefits are irrelevant to a technical presentation or that they are readily apparent. They often aren't, as they lie buried in technical jargon. Making the benefits link is seldom stating the obvious; instead, it results in clarity and persuasion.

Technical speakers also often assume a level of expertise—or vocabulary—in the audience that is just too high. Play it safe and never let your audience's level of education trick you into thinking you don't have to define your terms; make good analogies and clarify benefits. I once gave a talk to a high-level management group—or so I was told. I had prepared a speech that I thought would also be suitably high-level, but it quickly became apparent that my audience—mostly professional staff and new to management—wasn't following me. I quickly adjusted the speech before I had lost the audience's interest entirely.

Twenty-five Tricks of the Selling Trade

As a speaker you are a salesperson, and the item you're pushing is information. Your audience might be temporarily captive, but it isn't converted. You can sell your information more effectively if you remember people buy for emotional reasons, not factual ones. When you do give facts, try to tie them to the emotional needs of your audience.

Psychologist Abraham Maslow discovered that all people have a hierarchy of needs, and they rank from the most basic to the loftiest: physiological (sheer survival), security, social, self-esteem, and self-actualization—those rare moments when what we are doing and who we are seems exactly right. To sell through your speech or presentation you should keep these needs in the back of your mind, for they underlie the more obvious reasons people make decisions.

Here is by no means an exhaustive list of twenty-five reasons why people are persuaded to buy or say "yes" to something. You'll see that most relate directly to one of Maslow's steps in the hierarchy. Ask yourself if your speech ties in to at least one of these emotional needs.

1. To make money
2. To save money
3. To save time
4. To avoid effort
5. To gain comfort
6. To improve health
7. To escape pain
8. To be popular
9. To attract the opposite sex
10. To gain praise
11. To conserve our possessions
12. To increase our enjoyment
13. To satisfy curiosity

14. To protect our family
15. To be in style
16. To satisfy an appetite
17. To emulate others
18. To have beautiful things
19. To avoid criticism
20. To avoid trouble
21. To take advantage of opportunities
22. To be individual and unique
23. To protect our reputation
24. To gain control over aspects of our lives
25. To be safe

Get to Know Your Audience

You're trying to appeal to the members of your audience. Who are they? Generally speaking, they have needs, goals, troubles, and short attention spans. But what are those needs, goals, and troubles? Start your audience research by asking the following questions:

The Facts, Please
- Size of audience? Will you face an intimate group of ten around a table or a hall filled with bodies?
- Level of education?
- Age?
- Sex?
- Ethnic background? Religion?
- Political persuasion?
- How much time will you have to address the audience?
- What is the meeting's theme?
- Have other speakers addressed this audience on a similar topic?
- What do you think the audience's level of knowledge of the subject is?
- Will there be any VIPs, special guests, or press present?

The Setting
- What are the goals of the program chairman and the organization you're addressing?
- Are you the only speaker? If not, who is before you and who is after? Will their professional qualifications affect how you are perceived?
- What are the occupations of the members of your audience? Are people all in one industry or are they a diverse group?
- What is your group's special knowledge, purpose, and/or knowledge of your subject?
- What has the audience responded to most positively? Least positively?

The Audience Focus
- Analyze the occasion. Is it a special one, like an anniversary of the organization you're addressing?
- Specify the audience's needs and wants, current problems and concerns.
- What are your audience's primary interests and fixed ideas?
- Keep asking yourself: "What do I want my audience to know, do, and feel? Have I constructed my speech in such a way to make that happen?"

An Audience Aid

The forms included at the end of this chapter make it easy for you to get to know your audience. Use them before making your next presentation.

Be One of Them

More than anything, a well-prepared speaker is aware—not only of the audience's quirks and concerns but also of the larger picture: how current events may affect the presentation, what preconceived notions the members of the audience might have of the speaker's topic or reputation. But don't make the mistake of assuming your audience has knowledge about recent events such as the Korean War or the Vietnam War; a growing number of young people don't remember the assassination of President Kennedy because they were born after it. It's a fine line to walk: Although you shouldn't overestimate what your audience knows, you can't underestimate its knowledge, either.

Once you have constructed a speech that truly addresses your audience's needs, you're ready to add the basics—an opening, transitions, and a conclusion—that reinforce the importance of the material you are giving them.

Professional Project: Persuade Through Benefits

You are making a pitch for a raise. List three facts as to why you deserve it; along with the facts list the benefits that your boss will enjoy by granting it.

AUDIENCE ANALYSIS—PRELIMINARY: WHAT YOU NEED TO KNOW

1. Audience's major needs, problems, concerns at this moment?_____

2. Subject knowledge and vocabulary level?_____

3. Their relationship to me as speaker?_____

4. Level of education?_____

5. Age?_____

6. Sex? Ratio of men to women?_____

7. Ethnic background?_____

8. Occupation?_____

9. Audience size?_____

10. Any special interests or purpose of meeting?_____

11. Religion?_____

12. Political persuasion?_____

13. Special organization projects and current events?

    _____

14. Are there any other speakers before or after me on the program?_____

15. Will there be drinking or eating before my speech?

    _____

16. Have other speakers addressed this audience on a similar topic? Audience's reaction?_____

    _____

17. What has audience responded to most positively?___

_____

18. What has audience responded to least positively?___

_____

19. What data and support will persuade my audience, e.g., statistics, anecdotes, demonstrations, colorful visuals?_____

_____

Below is a questionnaire I have found works very well with clients who hire me to speak. Whether you have someone fill it out, or you research the information yourself, all these questions should be answered before you face your audience.

AUDIENCE ANALYSIS—CUSTOMIZED

This questionnaire is designed to help us prepare a program specifically suited to the needs of your group. Please take a moment to answer fully all the questions and return the form to our office. Thank you for your help!

Special Request: Please send all available printed material on your company, division, employees, and product/service line.

(If additional space is needed, use a blank sheet of paper and attach it to this questionnaire.)

1. What is the theme of your meeting?_____

   _____

2. What are the top three challenges or problems faced by the members of your group?

   (1) _____

   (2) _____

   (3) _____

3. What, approximately, are the characteristics of your average member?

   Age _____ Annual personal income _____

   Educational background _____

   Sex _____ Occupation _____

4. Will there be any special guests? Please explain

    _____

    _____

    _____

5. How many people will be in the audience?_____

6. Why is your group attending this meeting?_____

    _____

7. How will they be notified?_____

8. What is their overall opinion regarding the subject,
    e.g., favorable, hostile, etc. ?_____

    _____

9. What three facts should I know about your group
    before addressing them?

    (1) _____

    (2) _____

    (3) _____

10. What speakers have you used in the recent past and
    what did they discuss?

    (1) _____

    (2) _____

    (3) _____

11. What programs/speakers have been most enthusias-
    tically received?

    _____

_____

_____

12. Please list the names and positions of three people in the organization who are well known and well liked within the group, who will be present at the speech, and who I can joke with or call on if the need arises.

Name _____ Position_____

Name _____ Position_____

Name _____ Position_____

13. What are the three most significant events to have occurred in your industry, or within your group, during the past year?

(1) _____

(2) _____

(3) _____

14. Please share with me any "local color" you can think of relating to the location where my speech will be held.

_____

_____

_____

15. Please share with me any "industry color" you can think of relating to your organization or industry.

_____

_____

_____

16. Specifically, what are you trying to accomplish at this meeting?

   (1) _____

   (2) _____

   (3) _____

17. What are your specific objectives for my part of the meeting?

   (1) _____

   (2) _____

   (3) _____

18. Are there any issues/topics in particular that you think I should discuss during the program?

   (1) _____

   (2) _____

   (3) _____

19. Are there any issues/topics that you think I should avoid during the program?

   (1) _____

   (2) _____

   (3) _____

20. Do you have any suggestions to help me make this presentation the best your audience has ever heard?

   (1) _____

   (2) _____

   (3) _____

Part III

Conquering the

Trouble Spots:

The Basics—

Openings, Transitions,

and Conclusions

10

Starting on the Right

Foot: Openings That

Capture Your Audience

Things are always at their best in the beginning.
—Blaise Pascal

Powerful speakers start powerfully. You must gain the audience's attention and interest the moment you walk on the stage. Without that attention, you won't get your message across, you'll have trouble sustaining whatever interest there is, and you won't have established your leadership and control—the keys to being a powerful speaker.

As a speaker, you are an unknown quantity, but only for the first thirty seconds of your speech. After that, everything you say will be heard in the context of that first impression, those first sentences. So it's very important to memorize your opening and practice it many times. Since this is your first contact with your audience, you need to keep from looking down at your notes, which does not help you seem warm, powerful, or persuasive. Your eyes are the most important way to keep people's attention, so make sure you know your opening well.

Grab This Time of Heightened Expectations

At the start of your talk, you have a big attention advantage. You've been formally and perhaps enthusiastically introduced; the men and women at your presentation are hoping it will be interesting, hoping they will get something out of it, hoping it will not be a waste of their time. Your audience is in a state of expectation, and all you have to do is be reasonably confident, knowledgeable, and prepared *at the beginning*, and you'll have the audience on your side.

The opening is your appetizer; it is not meant to satisfy but to tempt, titillate, and arouse, and whet appetites for the next course. If you fail to get your audience's attention at the very beginning, it will take you at least three minutes to get it back, and people will already be less than excited about what is to come.

Compare these two openings:

1. "Um . . . hello, I'm your speaker, Dorothy Leeds, and I'm here to give some, or a few, clues on what foods to avoid so you can have less disease and less stress."

2. "Ladies and gentlemen: Would you like to add twenty quality years to your life? Then THINK before reaching for your salt shaker. I'm Dorothy Leeds, and I'm going to share with you ten easy, proven steps to add those twenty years to your life."

Years ago, the great architect Frank Lloyd Wright gave a speech in Pittsburgh. His attention-getting opening was "This is the ugliest city I have ever seen." Pittsburgh paid attention—to the opening and to the rest of the speech. In a recent survey the city was ranked as one of the most desirable places to live in the United States. Wright knew not to start out with "Good afternoon, it's a pleasure to be here," or with an irrelevant joke just for the sake of opening with humor. He came out swinging, and even if the people in the audience didn't agree with him, he had them listening.

Ten Opening Strategies

Openings have more crucial responsibilities than any other part of your speech. Although the following checklist may seem daunting, remember that one well-crafted opening can combine many tasks into just a few minutes or sentences. Getting attention is the key task of any opening, but it's not the extent of your opening's responsibilities. Here's a list of criteria for a powerful opening:

1. Get the audience's attention. How you get it is not nearly as important as making sure you do get it.
2. Build a bridge between what went on before and what is to come—your presentation. That's why people thank the introducer or refer back to previous speakers.
3. Let the audience know your purpose and objectives.
4. Get the members of your audience involved in your topic, your mission. You want their support, and you want them on your side.
5. Build expectations for what is to follow. Be careful about starting with a great joke you've practiced and then going into a list of facts and figures; your audience will feel let down.
6. Warm up those in your audience; relax them and show them they will have a good time listening to you, that you won't bore them. You're not putting them to sleep; you're saying, "It's OK, you're in good hands."
7. Give the listeners confidence in you by showing how they will profit from and enjoy what they're about to hear.
8. Let the audience know you are in control. Give any necessary directions, such as how and when you will deal with questions or handouts. Explain everything up front.
9. Disclose something about yourself to further gain the

audience's support by showing that you are human, fallible, or whatever is appropriate to the occasion.
10. Let the people in the audience know you're glad to be
with them. This can be evident from your own enthusiasm; you can also address a compliment directly to the
members of your audience, or disclose something about
yourself in a way that shows you are relaxed around them.

Openings have to do a lot, but speakers have great free-
dom in crafting them—an advantage other writers, like
playwrights and novelists, lack. You don't have to confine
your story to a character's personality or to history. You
can use all kinds of visual and audio aids. You don't have
to keep the action tied to a specific place and time. You
can roam from past to present to future, all in one sentence. You can draw your sources from almost any context. Above all, you can adjust and tailor your message to
the specific audience you're addressing.

Easy Ways to Get Attention—Quickly

All this leeway means the criteria for a good opening con-
sist of one question: Does it grab the audience's attention?
It's like the tree falling in the forest: Does it make a sound
if no one is there to hear it? You may be up on a platform,
ready to speak, but without your audience's attention, the
speech will reach deaf ears.

Although a lot of your opening success comes down to
your delivery style, and the passion you bring to your subject, the fourteen devices listed below can be especially
effective when incorporated into your opening:

■ *Audience compliment.* Don't use sheer flattery with no
relevant purpose, but insert a sincere comment on some
positive quality of the people before you. You want them
to like you; show you already like them. I often use the

following comment when I'm speaking: "I'm especially pleased to be here today, because I totally agree with the five-foot, six-inch Kansas City shortstop who said, 'I'd rather be the shortest player in the majors than the tallest one in the minors.' " (This works well since I am 5'1".)

▣ *Questions and rhetorical questions.* As the author of *Smart Questions: A New Strategy for Successful Managers*, I am a strong believer in the power of questions. Direct questions also get your audience involved—the key to a good opening. Staff and motivational speakers often use them because people will pay more attention to things they think of rather than to what you put forth.

By asking a rhetorical question, you can restate your point in a dramatic way. Rhetorical questions make people think. After a presentation where I discuss the power and effectiveness of asking questions, I ask, "If questions are so powerful, why don't we use them more?" These questions can involve your audience and get people to think about the answer in their own minds. You focus their attention without engaging in the give-and-take of a true question-and-answer session.

Before you incorporate a question, analyze it for rhetorical effect: Will it make your audience think? Will it get them mentally—and even physically—involved.

▣ *Startling statement or statistic.* Combine brevity with a degree of shock—two powerful qualities for any opening—by leading off with a startling statement or statistic. Be careful not to use too many at once, since people only remember one or two at a time.

▣ *Joke.* Many people feel they have to start with a joke, perhaps because they have heard so many other speakers do so. But as I mentioned earlier, you must be careful about setting up expectations of more jokes to come. The best time to use a joke is if it fits in with your topic just beautifully and you can tell it well, or if you intend to intersperse jokes throughout the speech.

Even with the risks, jokes can be a very good way to begin. I once attended a presentation on tunnel vision—a topic that can easily slip into predictable admonishments. The speaker began by telling a joke about two ostriches running away from two other ostriches. They couldn't run fast enough, so they decided to hide. She then looked at the audience and said, "Do you know how ostriches hide? Do you know how vulnerable you are in that position?" The audience chuckled, and she had made her point—that tunnel vision can be disastrous—effectively.

■ *Visual aid.* Visual aids can get attention quickly. I once saw a presentation on the advantages of nuclear power where the speaker held up a picture of a smiling Arab holding oil and U.S. dollars in his hands. Instantly, the speaker had made his point about nuclear power freeing us from some of the expense of importing.

■ *Personal experience.* Starting with a relevant story about yourself establishes empathy and rapport, and also confirms your qualifications to address the topic.

■ *Reference to an occasion.* If you are addressing the one hundredth anniversary of an association, work it into your opening. Your speech will instantly seem tailor-made for the members of the group, and they will sense what's coming up will also focus on them.

■ *Reference to a current event.* Few speeches are given in a void; show off the links between your topic and the world at large. Doing so gives the audience a larger context in which to listen and to remember your words. Try to avoid being overly controversial, since you never know the current mind-set of your audience.

■ *Quotation.* Quotations are popular and with reason: The hard-earned wisdom of renowned people tends to be succinct, witty, and memorable. And a quotation can focus the attention of your audience much faster than traditional exposition.

■ *Citing an authority.* You can often gain attention if you align yourself with a higher authority, whether it's a prize-winning scientist or the head of your department.

■ *Audience challenge.* Don't be afraid to startle people; conflict is at the center of every successful play, and it can work equally well in a talk. You involve people even if they don't agree with you. Just make sure your challenge to the audience relates to the subject of the speech; otherwise, it will seem inappropriate. I use this challenge in my training sessions with managers improving their communication skills: "I dare you to put me out of business!"

■ *Story.* Make your opening come alive by telling a story; stories tend to be things audiences remember with ease. John F. Kennedy told a story about a taxi ride before his election. He got out and was about to tip lavishly and tell the cabbie to vote Democratic. Then he remembered some advice from his father. He got out of the cab, didn't tip at all, and told the cabbie to vote Republican.

■ *Comparison.* Comparisons are especially vivid if they relate to some daily aspect of your audience's life. I have heard cost-of-living expenses used to point out disparities between different parts of the country.

■ *An unusual definition.* These definitions are everywhere, and you can find the best ones in anthologies and quotation books. An example: "Men are like cellophane: hard to get rid of once you get wrapped in them." The more vivid the definition is, the more your audience will remember it.

Openings to Avoid

Just as there are ways to grab an audience's attention, there are traps even experienced speakers fall into that work swiftly to halt whatever momentum you're building:

■ *Don't use the opening to restate the title of the speech or to reiterate information.* You need every moment to create interest and suspense; don't go over what is already known. Don't start by saying "I am going to talk to you today about . . . safety."

■ *Don't open your speech with an apology.* You may think it makes you sound friendly and not pompous, but apologies set up your audience to listen for your weaknesses.

■ *Don't greet the "important" people in the audience.* Forget saying "Thank you, Mr. Chairman, Mayor Jones, Senator Smith, . . ." The only time you would use such a formal opening is as a political candidate speaking before a very distinguished audience. If you want to bring attention to certain people in the audience, use their names in the context of your speech.

■ *Don't explain your presence.* Don't offer explanations about why you *think* the chairman asked you to address the group. Remember that you are there for a good reason; you know it, and the audience knows it. Also remember the maxim covering explanations: "Your friends don't need it, and your enemies won't believe you anyway."

■ *Don't say how difficult it was to choose the subject.* As far as the audience is concerned, your topic should be so vital that you never doubted its importance, and you should communicate that vital nature.

Hook your listeners at the outset, and you're well on your way to winning the battle for their attention. At the very least, like a good suspense novelist, you will have aroused enough curiosity that they will want to see what comes next.

Professional Projects: Sharpen Your Openings

1. Develop an opening of 250 to 450 words that includes at least eight elements of an effective opening. This

should be the opening for an informative speech that serves as an orientation to your department for new employees.

2. Your topic is "We Can Beat Inflation." Devise four different openings using the following attention-getters: a joke, a rhetorical question, a startling statistic, and a personal story.

11

Bridging the Gap: Building

Smooth Transitions

Good transitions can make a speech more important to the audience because they feel they are being taken to a positive conclusion without having to travel a bumpy road.
—Joe Griffith

Transitions are what make an average speech seem polished and professional. When I tell participants in my speaking classes that overlooked transitions are one of public speaking's most common problems, I can see the look of collective recognition as people remember the moments when they paused and stammered because they didn't know how to get from point *A* to point *B*.

While an attention-getting opening is crucial to the beginning of a speech, the challenge is to keep the ideas that follow just as vivid. Yet many speakers concentrate all their ammunition on the opening, thinking that with a strong start, the rest can just follow. Not true. Your audience understands every new idea only if it relates to other ideas or experiences.

So you can't just present ideas; you must *lead* your audience. And that's where transitions come in; they are the maps you use when you are leading a group and you need to tell them which direction to go in next. The better organized you are, the easier it will be for you to develop smooth transitions. And the leadership evidenced when you're clearly in control adds to your power as a presenter.

Transitions: The Often Forgotten Basic

As we've learned, speeches are made up of many parts that must fit well together. And transitions are responsible for much of that fitting: They take you from your opening into the body of your speech and provide a smooth passage between your main points, while also serving as smaller links between minor ideas. Yet transitions are so useful and frequent that they are often overlooked. If you hear a speaker stumble, chances are it's over a transition. Novice speakers shift gears using "um," "ah," and phrases like "let's see . . . our next point is. . . ." Look at your outline for a speech and see how many topics and subtopics you have. Each one requires a transition before you plunge your audience into it.

Successful Transition Techniques

It's always a good idea to memorize your transitions, or to write them clearly on the notecards you will have with you during your speech. Label these cards "transition cards" so you know when they are coming and can get ready to shift gears.

Frequent transitions carry your story forward, and they also help you to keep the audience's attention from drooping by strengthening logic, aiding retention, and helping you build to a climax. Frequent transitions add peaks to the curve of your speech and keep it interesting. The best ones will lead your audience in a subtle and natural way. You don't want your audience to feel it is being led, but you do want it to be alerted to new points you are about to introduce.

I once heard a speaker trying to persuade his audience to exercise; he used this transition into his conclusion: "And so, ladies and gentlemen, why exercise?" He then listed all the terrible consequences of inactivity and then said quietly, "The quality and quantity of the rest of your life is up to you." It was very effective.

Don't be afraid to use physical movements that reinforce your transitions. When this speaker on exercise reached the concluding transition I described above, he also moved from one side of the stage to the other, which emphasized the shift he was making as he spoke.

The important thing is to spot where you need transitions. A rule of thumb is to use one any time you finish a thought and are ready to move on to a new idea. Major shifts—where your topic is really changing or you are introducing a new area—require unmistakable transitions. Give yourself at least a sentence to bring this shift to your audience's attention.

Transitions are Meant to Be Noticed

In writing, transitions are subtle. The knitting together of character, thoughts, and action into a narrative should be almost invisible. But in a speech, transitions that bridge the gaps from one topic to another are much more obvious because you have to be sure your listeners cross the bridge with you. If the transition is too subtle, they may miss it and remain on topic *A*, while you are well launched into topic *B*. An effective transition always lets the audience know you are moving from one point to another. The process can be straightforward or creative, depending on the device you use.

Ten Transitions That Work

Good speakers vary their transition style and avoid being predictable.

Here are ten types of transitions that are easy to use:

1. The simplest transitions are *bridge words*—words that alert the listener that you are changing direction or moving on to a new thought. Examples of bridge words include: furthermore, meanwhile, however, in addition, nevertheless, moreover, therefore, consequently, and finally.

2. A *trigger transition* relies on repetition, using the same word twice to connect one topic with the next. "That wraps up our assessment of product *A*. A similar assessment can be made of product *B*" is an example of this type of transition.

3. A *question* can serve as a good transition. It can be broad or quite specific. At a seminar on productivity, I shifted people's attention by saying, "Now that we have seen what an effective team is, what can we do to *build* that better team within this organization?" It was a large question that I was about to address one part at a time, using smaller transitions between those parts.

4. A *flashback* can be a transition and can also create movement within your talk with its sudden shift to the past in the midst of what the audience may think is a predictable sequence. The flashback doesn't have to be far in the past; use a transition like "You remember that I mentioned the major changes in our work force a few minutes ago . . . another example of the dramatic changes we will face this year is. . . ."

Flashbacks can serve as minisummaries sprinkled throughout a speech. They are especially helpful transitions because they aid your listeners in remembering your ideas and seeing how everything fits together. They also let you build your argument by summoning the points you have made before. A simple example is "So far we've talked about hiring new people and training our existing staff. Another possibility is a reorganization that would . . ."

5. A *point-by-point* transition can also work, if you don't have too many points. Saying "There are three important reasons this product will sell in the Midwest" and then listing them is a quick way to shift from generalities into specificity. These transitions can also serve as miniconclusions that sum up what you have said in a previous section of your speech.

Be careful not to overuse point-by-point transitions, since they are the least dynamic and can easily bore audiences unless you have lots of lively examples with emotional appeal. Good visual aids also liven up a presentation that depends on point-by-point transitions.

6. *Visual aids* are transitional by their very nature. Shifting from unaided speech to the mechanics of visual aids carries a built-in transition, as you turn down lights or start to use whatever equipment you have chosen. And when you use visual aids to illuminate complex points quickly and vividly (instead of just using slides to restate what you could easily convey verbally), you are making visual aids a transition that also enlightens.

7. *Pausing* is a nonverbal transition that helps your audience shift with you. Good use of a pause—if done sparingly—helps your listeners focus on what you are about to say. But be careful—too many pauses will make your delivery seem frustratingly slow and stilted.

8. *Physical movement*—such as moving to another part of a platform—also acts as a transition between parts of your speech. As I mentioned, just shifting from one prop or visual aid to another is its own transition, since it refocuses the audience.

Effective nonverbal transitions entail doing the opposite of what your audience has gotten used to. If you have been pacing, suddenly stand still. If you have been standing in one place behind a lectern, move about suddenly. Either way, you call attention to what is about to come—which is the essence of a good transition.

9. A *joke* or a *story* can act as an interesting transition. In a talk to managers on why and how to become better listeners, I used the Epictetus quotation, "God has given us two ears and one mouth—so we may hear twice as much as we speak." I added: "Now, since people talk twice as much as they listen, we must reverse the process and listen twice as much as we talk.'' The quotation helped me make my point and provided a way for me to shift to my next idea.

10. The *PEP formula*—Point, Example, Point—is a valuable transition in itself, because it makes connections between points for your audience.

Transitions are the seams that keep the parts of your speech fitting smoothly. They let you take the audience by the hand and guide it in the direction you want to go, and they also reinforce your main points.

Mastering transitions means realizing the best ones are frequent, varied, clear, and compelling. Transitions turn an outline, with its abrupt switches, into a smooth, memorable presentation—and turn you into a persuasive, powerful presenter.

Professional Project: Tackling Transitions

You are giving a talk titled ''Elephants Don't Bite.'' And your very serious purpose is to get your department to economize on the little things that add up to big expenses. Your opening will explain the title and state your purpose. Write the transition that leads from the opening into the body of your talk.

12

Finishing with Style:

The Importance of

Powerful Conclusions

Great is the art of beginning, but greater the art is of ending.   —Henry Wadsworth Longfellow

You've grabbed attention in the opening, sustained it through the transitions, and now all you have to do is close. It may seem like a time to wind down, to simply sum up and breathe a sigh of relief. And, of course, it's not. For no matter how vivid the words that came before, your conclusion is your prime time; it's what your whole speech should build toward. Don't throw it away. Instead, build up to it, and make sure it is stimulating and memorable.

People tend to remember more about the last thing they hear than about the middle of a talk. Yet the majority of speakers just fade away when they get to the end of their speeches. I've seen people so relieved their stint on the podium is over, they start to pack up before they finish speaking. Powerful speakers save a lot of energy and concern for the audience until the end, and make the conclusion their dessert: something delicious, with a memorable aftertaste.

Fitting Conclusions Don't Just Happen

The best time to prepare your conclusion is when you begin thinking about your speech. Memorize and practice your conclusion just as you do for your opening. Your conclusion must tie in with your opening and your overall purpose; it's an ending that must connect naturally with your beginning, and that's where organization continues to be important. Conclusions are your destination: You begin a speech where your audience is, but you end where *you* want them to be. The body of the speech is a bridge, and the speaker must always know what that bridge links. Always conclude with your own ideas, especially after a question-and-answer session. Alert the audience in the beginning of your speech that you will reserve the last few minutes to tie things up.

But don't announce your intention to conclude. If people get a lot of advance warning that you are going to conclude, they wind up your speech in their mind and start to tune you out. Be more subtle: Lead into your conclusion with a creative transition instead of the not very dynamic "and so, in conclusion, I would like to point out . . ." A good conclusion needs a lot of energy: It may be a stirring statement, a joke, a call to action. Some conclusions try to motivate through a challenge issued directly to the audience.

I once heard an executive outlining new organizational changes after a takeover. Predictably, the members of his audience were nervous, and rumors of layoffs were rampant. He described the changes and ended his presentation by saying, "I dare you to come in tomorrow, to put aside your fears and apprehensions and to give your all." That direct challenge to the unspoken reservations the members held roused them and let him end on a strong, memorable, and positive note.

A fund-raiser ended a speech by saying, "How can you go home tonight and sleep with a clear conscience, knowing there are hungry children in this world? Dig into your pockets and dig deep.'' Almost everyone in the audience did just that.

Ask for the Order

A good sales pitch will not only ask people to order but also tell them how. When you buy a car, the dealer explains the auto's features, points out why it is better than the one you already own, and *then* tells you how you can pay for it.

Speakers, as you now know, are also in the selling business, and the conclusion is the time to ask for the order. Nothing will happen if you don't ask. And you ask by telling your audience what you want it to do with the information you've presented and *how* it can take that action. An effective speaker presenting a central idea ends by pointing out to those in his audience exactly what is needed from them to put that idea to work. For example, if you have been talking about on-the-job safety, end with an emotional and specific appeal showing why safety is important to the people in front of you, and how they can ensure safe operations by applying the information you've presented. If you've been persuading them to give blood, tell them where. And make it sound easy to get there.

Getting a visible demonstration of support is an effective technique. If you shared with your staff ten reasons why they must operate their vehicles in a specific manner, end by telling them how lives could be saved, including theirs. End by asking, then and there, for a show of hands from those committed to the new procedures. This is not the time to be shy, but to be rousing.

Action doesn't always have to be literal. If you simply want the people in your audience to mull over your ideas, tell them this is what you want them to do. Summarize your important thoughts in sequence; in doing so, you give them a verbal pocket digest they can carry away with them. If you fail to ask for a specific action, you may end up giving a wonderful speech that builds up to—nothing.

One way to zero in on a dynamic closing is to ask yourself, "What do I want the members of my audience to think about as they leave?" Remember that the conclusion is not a second chance: If you've failed to get your ideas across in the body of your talk, it's too late now. You've presented your message; now is the time to fix that message in your listener's minds.

Six Aids to Strong Endings

Your closing statement should be brief yet strong. There are six major devices for concluding your talk. You can use each alone, or combine them with the others. In addition, the devices for openings, transitions, and closings are very similar, and the same device can be used in numerous places.

1. Summarize your major ideas. Conclusions should contain a summary. Don't make it a total rehash; instead, add some new thoughts or elements and a final statement. A summary is especially effective if the primary purpose of your talk is to give information. By restating your ideas you may fill in some blanks for listeners who didn't fully grasp or respond to your entire presentation. But don't repeat yourself at length. Look for a fresh way of summing up and emphasize only the essential.

2. Make a direct appeal. You have told the people in your audience what you want them to do and why and how. Now stir them to action with a ringing declaration or challenge. This can be as simple as saying, in a rousing tone, "Now let's get up and make this work!"

3. Look ahead. You may want to close with a prediction that holds forth hope and promise of better things to come. So turn your audience's thoughts to the future. If your talk has focused on disastrous corporate events, find some positive alternatives to end with. A talk on reshaping a marketing division could end, ''With this new advertising approach, we can avoid the losses facing our industry, and next year we will be able to see black instead of red.''

4. Ask a rhetorical question. This device lets people fill in the answer for themselves, and you can combine it with other methods of closing. During a talk on safety, a rhetorical question might be, ''Do you want to be the next statistic?'' These questions make your speech a two-way street by actively inviting the audience's mental participation. They allow you to steer the audience's response in your direction. And while many rhetorical questions have evident answers, that very obviousness can give them a vividness and sense of urgency.

5. Refer back to your opening comments. Doing this ties your whole speech together. Your audience sees your talk as a satisfying whole, rather than a series of points without any particular direction.

I once heard an executive conclude simply—and very effectively—with her opening words: ''Now really is the time for all good people to come to the aid of their company.'' Opening statements often refer to the purpose of the talk, and conclusions that return to and reinforce that purpose can make effective endings. A speech on customer service started with the advice to treat the customer the way you would want to be treated and ended with the speaker asking the members of the audience to think back and remember how they felt when they were customers and were treated rudely.

6. Conclude your speech with a quotation. An appropriate quotation can conclude many kinds of talks and provides a graceful ending. Quotations also let you borrow the prestige of a higher source and help to crystallize the audience's thinking.

Sources for stirring summations are no farther away than a good directory of quotations. Voltaire was succinct when he said, "No problem can withstand the assault of sustained thinking." A seminar on hiring could end on a good note with this bit of wisdom from R. H. Rands: "When you hire people smarter than you are, you prove that you are smarter than they are." John Charles Salak defined failure two ways, with particular pertinence to business, when he said there were two kinds of failures: those who thought and never did and those who did and never thought. Persistence, motivation, generosity, the rewards of hard work—all these universal topics have been addressed by eloquent people, and their words are yours to use to great effect.

Combine Closing Techniques

Many conclusions will borrow from a combination of the above techniques. A fund-raising presentation I attended had a three-part conclusion: It started with a summary of reasons why the cause was especially worthy and led into this quotation from Ralph Waldo Emerson: "No man can truly help another man without helping himself." The speaker then launched into a direct appeal: "So please reach into your hearts and checkbooks so that tomorrow really will be a better day for the needy."

These techniques also apply in general communication. For example, after a meeting with a client you might need to sum up your discussion or ask for the order. Never let important conversations or discussions just drift away.

Whatever technique you use, strive for a conclusion that will stay with your listeners long after they leave their seats and return to their private lives. The conclusion is the last "basic"; you're now ready to start polishing as we move on to the fine points of PowerSpeak.

Professional Project:
Concentrate on Conclusions

You are a Boy or Girl Scout troop leader on a day-long swimming trip. You've given a talk about the importance of the "buddy system." End by summarizing your key points and include a strong call to action.

Part IV

Mastering the

Fine Points

of Powerful Speaking

13

Power Language:

Turning Everyday

Words into Persuasion

Poetry is ordinary language raised to the nth power.
—Paul Engle

What's the difference between a pleasant, serviceable speech and a great one? Between a speech that does the job and one that makes your heart beat faster? A speech that you listen to politely, and one that persuades you to change your thinking?

By now you know enough to go out and give a good working speech. But why stop at the basics? It's only a few steps more to a speech that has the power to persuade and influence your listeners. The difference between a good speech and a great speech is *language*.

But don't panic. By language I don't mean grammar or vocabulary but the way you use simple, everyday language. This chapter will show you some of the best ways to make your everyday language both eloquent and persuasive.

Avoid the Passive Voice

Choosing the active voice—instead of the passive voice—is your most important step to a powerful speech. The active voice relies on *verbs*. "The boy ran" is more powerful than "the boy was seen running." The active voice has a clear subject, and in speeches that subject is usually *you*. You take responsibility by saying "I saw," or "I believe." The passive and impersonal "It has been seen that," rather than "I saw," may remove you from the line of fire, but it makes for boring speeches. If Caesar had spoken that way, his powerful *Veni, Vidi, Vici"* ("I came, I saw, I conquered") would have been: "The place was arrived at, was observed, and was duly overtaken."

One way to keep your language active is to eliminate verbs that end in *"-ing."* "I run" is stronger than "I am running." A title such as "How to Run a Meeting" is stronger than "Running a Meeting."

Modifiers Sap Your Strength

Powerful speeches eliminate the words and phrases that weaken language. And these little phrases are everywhere: People use "perhaps" and "I think that maybe" almost without realizing it. Powerless speakers use "It seems like" and "you know." Their language is filled with modifiers like "kind of" and "sort of." Compare the difference between saying "I hope I can get that done for you" and "I know I can get that done for you." One little word can make a great difference. If you feel strongly about something, use strong words. "I think" is not strong. It automatically weakens what follows, even though what usually follows is an assertion. "This is the best solution" is much stronger than "I think this is the best solution."

Social scientists at Duke University have been able to pinpoint a specific pattern that identifies powerless speech. Intensifiers like *very, definitely,* and *surely* do the opposite of what they are supposed to do: They weaken the descriptive adjective that follows by not letting it stand on its own. "The car is fast" is a stronger statement than "The car is very fast."

Powerless speakers also hesitate often, relying on fillers

like "uh," "umm," and "well . . ." to get them from point to point. They are overly polite, and often use "sir" and "please." Obviously politeness has its place, but if you are too polite you seem timid and worried that what you are going to say will offend. And if *you* seem to have doubts about what you have to say about your subject, your audience won't be far behind.

Beware the Ponderous Trap

Modifiers may weaken language to the point of forgettable speech, but equally bad is the style of speech politicians and social scientists adopt when they're cornered or simply trying to impress. I call it *babblespeak*. The essence of this style is using a lot of words that say as little as possible. Unfortunately, this tendency isn't limited to specialists; many people feel they must use big words to make an impression, when in reality, vivid language is simple and direct.

The good platform speaker avoids this babbling style like poison. To avoid becoming a babbler:

- Always use a single syllable word instead of a word with three syllables or more.
- Always use one word to make your point instead of three; use common words instead of stilted words and jargon.
- Never be passive: Use lots of active verbs and stay away from nouns and prepositions. Always commit yourself.
- Never beat around the bush; say everything straight out.

Much of this cloudy language has bureaucratic sources. A plumber in New York wrote to the Bureau of Standards in Washington. He said that he found hydrochloric acid was great for cleaning drains, but was it safe? A bureaucrat answered: "The efficacy of hydrochloric acid is indisputable, but the chlorine residue is incompatible with metallic permanence.''

The plumber replied he was glad that Washington thought he was right. He got another reply: ''We cannot assume responsibility for the production of toxic and noxious residues with hydrochloric acid.'' Right, the plumber answered, it's good stuff.

Finally, the Bureau sent the plumber a note saying what it had meant all along: ''Don't use hydrochloric acid; it eats the hell out of the pipes!''

The worst thing about this sort of babble is that once you start, it's very easy to fall into its trap. One complicated sentence leads to another and before long, you have a whole speech—but it will be one that audiences will have a tough time listening to.

Use Words That Are Right for You

Let me emphasize a point I made earlier: Anyone—regardless of his or her vocabulary—can be an outstanding speaker. You don't have to know unusual or complicated words to use power language. The important thing is to use language that is comfortable for you and to use it in a creative, colorful way.

If you do use complicated words, make sure they're completely familiar to you. The president of a football team forgot this rule when he introduced a recently acquired player: ''His influence on the state's economy will be inconceivable,'' he crowed. Then he thought a bit. ''I mean incontrovertible. No . . . inconsequential. Well, here he is.'' Misusing a word in an attempt to appear learned has led many speakers into the land of Mrs. Malaprop: ''My wife tells me I'm an invertebrate smoker.''

Sometimes a slip of the tongue is good for a laugh. Kenneth Keating was once invited to give a speech with this charming invitation: ''I hope you can come, Senator, because we would all like to hear the dope from Washington.'' Senator Keating turned that into a classic story and used it repeatedly in future speeches. Will Rogers was one gifted speaker who used the wrong word on purpose very effectively: ''In some states they no longer hang murderers—they kill them by elocution.'' In both cases, the speaker used a word that surprised, and that came at the end of a sentence—a perfect combination for memorable sentences.

Watch Where You Put Your Words

Power comes from powerful phrases; it also comes from knowing where to put those phrases. Good speakers use an influential technique used by trial lawyers—people who sway audiences for high stakes. It's called *the doctrine of primacy and recency*, and it refers to people's tendency to remember beginnings and endings.

Given this tendency in listeners, effective speakers will put their crucial information at the beginning and end of each sentence, and paragraph, for the entire speech. Whatever comes in the middle tends to get lost. Listeners' concentration is high with the first word, wavers as a statement continues, and is high again with the last word or phrase. If you say the sentence ''My boss is fair, observant, considerate, and generous,'' people will remember *fair* and *generous*. An evocative exception to this rule are phrases or lists with three parts: ''I came, I saw, I conquered'' uses the natural rhythm found in trinities. Listen to comics and humorists, whose deliveries often take advantage of the rhythmic properties of balanced sentences.

There is no universal agreement about which position— the beginning or the end—is the most powerful. The doctrine of primacy says lead off with your strongest statement. The recency argument says finish with your most powerful punch. Usually it's a matter of using your strongest point in one place, and your next strongest in the other.

Words That Reverberate

There are two components to creating powerful language: eliminating the words that detract from your message and adding language that, although ordinary, resonates. Great speakers use language the same way songwriters do: They use imagery to create mental pictures, repetition to make ideas stick in your mind, and rhythm to stir your emotions.

The key to power language is to recognize that words have something more than their basic meaning; they have emotional content, too. And it's the emotion you're going for. Henry James said the most beautiful words in the English language were *summer afternoon*. Those two simple words convey a nostalgic picture to almost everyone. And the picture is universally pleasant since most people will remember one idyllic summer's day at the seashore or the ball game, rather than a sweltering journey in a crowded train or bus. The words *summer afternoon* simply make you feel good.

Even the *sound* of certain words convey more than meaning. The word *buzz* not only means a whirring sound but also sounds like one. *Bombastic, bamboozles, blunderbuss, nincompoop, lackadaisical, rambunctious, scalawag*—all sound just like their definitions.

Aim for the Emotions

Fear, love, anger, compassion—they all have the power to stir anyone in front of you. If you want to influence your audience you must search for language that has emotional appeal. These appeals don't have to be blatant and obvious; in fact, the best ones are subtle. You can create emotional appeals by using impact phrases: memorable groups of words that shake listeners from lethargy and stay in their minds. Ideally, these phrases touch basic human emotions and help your listeners empathize with your perspective. A fund-raiser for the homeless says, "Think how you would feel if you had no home. . . ." An opponent of airline deregulation asks, "Remember how angry you felt the last time your plane got canceled, or you sat on the runway for hours?"

When Abraham Lincoln finished the Gettysburg Address, many listeners had tears in their eyes. But tears are not the only, or even the most important, measure of emotional impact. Laughter is also a basic emotion, and impact phrases can be humorous. Describing his own tendency to procrastinate, one speaker said, "I am rather like a mosquito in a nudist camp: I know what I ought to do, but I don't know where to begin."

Never underestimate rhetoric's ability to move an audience; it's been doing just that for centuries. Gorgias, a Greek who lived in the fourth century B.C., was renowned in Athens for using language so beautiful people thought it was magic. Three centuries earlier, Archilochus, another master of words, had a reputation for caustic phrases. After he spoke witheringly of his in-laws one day, they were so upset by his words that they killed themselves. Although the average businessperson no doubt has less severe reactions in mind, it's good to realize nonetheless that words can and do go straight for the emotions, even in the most routine presentation. Memorable speakers harness the inherent power of words.

The Twelve Most Persuasive Words in the English Language

While you're aiming for the emotions, you'll find these words coming to your aid over and over again.

1. *Discovery.* With shades of childhood treasures, this word conveys excitement and adventure. If you tell the people in your audience that you want to share a discovery with them, you start to make your enthusiasm contagious.
2. *Easy.* Many people are basically lazy and will look for

a quick, uncomplicated answer. The success of Kenneth Blanchard and Spencer Johnson's book *The One-Minute Manager* is proof of this tendency.

3. *Guarantee.* We are all reluctant to try something new because of the risk involved. Take away that fear by guaranteeing a sure thing, and you can sell your audience on the point you're trying to make.

4. *Health.* Self-preservation is a great motivator. We gravitate toward anything that will improve our condition or make us feel better.

5. *Love.* The thing we can't do without, and the one word that evokes all kinds of romantic fantasies.

6. *Money.* People react perceptibly at the thought of making money.

7. *New.* Having something new, knowing something new—this word has an intrinsic appeal. Speakers are always striving to make their presentations impart new facts and figures.

8. *Proven.* Another no-risk word. *Proven* assures listeners that something has already been tested and given the go-ahead.

9. *Results.* This is the bottom line—where you tell people about what they will get, what will happen, and so on.

10. *Safety.* Unless your audience has a death wish, the idea of safety is very comforting.

11. *Save.* Even the wealthiest people shop for bargains. It's not just money that entices; people also want to hear about saving time.

12. *You.* I've saved the most important word for last. Persuasive speakers personalize their talks and use this word often. Try to avoid personal pronouns—I, we, our—and the anonymity of "today's session." Make it "*your* session today," and carry that emphasis on *your* throughout your presentation. You can't stir your audience up if you don't address it directly.

Power expressions join power words in their ability to command attention—whether overtly or subliminally. The phrases that follow pique listeners' interest and keep them listening for what's to come: "Here's how you will benefit." "Here are the results you have been waiting for." "This will answer your questions." "I have a new plan to put before you." "You will discover how you can . . ."

Reach for Vivid Comparisons

All impact phrases use imagery. Imagery helps your listeners understand and remember. When you want to explain an idea, draw a mental picture and then color it in. Your job as a speaker is to get people to imagine, think, and *feel.* Saying something longed for was as "welcome as a glass of cool water after eating a very hot pepper" isn't just unexpected; it conjures up taste, heat, relief, and refreshment in your listeners' minds. Speakers have many verbal tools to paint pictures with, and two of the best are *metaphors* and *similes.*

These two popular figures of speech are similar to each other, and most speakers don't find it necessary to distinguish between them. Certainly their purpose is the same: to create a striking, vivid picture with few words. Metaphors and similes transfer the image of one thing to another. "Man is still the most extraordinary computer of all," is the metaphor John F. Kennedy used to describe L. Gordon Cooper. These devices are fast and effective. Ralph Waldo Emerson's "Hitch your wagon to a star" conveys instant advice to the ambitious and to dreamers.

When you do create a metaphor or simile, make sure it is appropriate to your audience and style. And do your best to make it original. A worn-out cliché—"dead as a doornail" or "white as a sheet"—is weak. We have heard it so often it no longer has impact. Original figures of speech are the ones that attract attention and make the image stick in your listeners' minds. One speaker trying to duck hostile questions at a news conference said, "I

somehow feel there's a boomerang loose in the room."
That's a good, original metaphor.

Try not to mix up your images. "Now that Jim is back
in the saddle, everything will be smooth sailing" is a
mixed metaphor that paints a confusing picture of cowboys
on the high seas.

A simile is a more direct, less subtle version of a metaphor. It also compares unlike things, usually with con-
necting words such as *like, as,* or *is.* "Power is poison"
is a short, sharp simile. "He keeps himself in the public
eye like a cinder" is a perfect, ear-catching simile. Here's
a vivid one: Truman Capote once said that "Venice is like
eating an entire box of chocolate liqueurs in one go."

People use metaphors and similes in virtually every
speaking situation. Charles de Gaulle used one to make a
political statement: "Treaties are like roses and young
girls. They last while they last." I once heard a woman
address a group for the second time; she said, "My stories
are like good wine and good women—they improve with
age."

Another useful figure of speech that creates magnificent
imagery is hyperbole, which is purposeful exaggeration.
"He could sell refrigerators to Eskimos" is a classic example. When Dorothy Parker shared office space with
Robert Benchley she said they had an office "so tiny that
an inch smaller and it would have been adultery."

Apt Analogies

One of the most useful figures of speech for platform
speakers, an analogy lets you quickly explain a new idea
by comparing it with something familiar and simple. Ben-
jamin Franklin said, "Fish and visitors start to smell in
three days," and gave a concise picture of why people
should not overstay their welcomes.

Analogies are especially useful for speakers who have
to present technical or scientific information. By compar-

ing the complex with something ordinary and familiar, your listeners understand by association. One speaker effectively explained a computer by comparing it with a secretary. The essayist Lewis Thomas explained the universe by comparing it with the life of a single cell. There are many other figures of speech that speakers use to create powerful images—parables, fables, epithets, icons, and personifications, to name a few.

Other Tricks of the Language

Other colorful devices can get attention. Sound makes a strong impression, and speakers often use alliteration (using several words that begin with the same letter) to implant a phrase in the collective mind of the audience. I used alliteration in the title of this book. Winston Churchill was a master of alliteration: "He was a man of light and learning." "We cannot fail or falter." Listeners can remember those phrases because of the alliteration and also because the nouns and verbs are simple and direct. These phrases also persuade.

Repetition is another powerful speaking device. George M. Cohan created one of the most stirring and memorable calls to action through the exclusive use of repetition: "Over there, over there . . . the Yanks are coming, the Yanks are coming, the drums drum drumming everywhere . . . So beware, so beware. . . ." The cadence—or rhythm—of language also has an emotional pull. Churchill used cadence to create a stirring image: "Let us to the task, to the battle, to the toil."

Borrowing Eloquence

The trend in today's public speaking is much more conversational than the arm-waving oratory of old. Even so, powerful speech is often eloquent. A few select, powerful phrases in a speech can be the spice needed to make what you say memorable, rather than just easy to listen to.

One way to achieve eloquence is to quote from those who have been eloquent before you. When Sir Isaac Newton was asked how he saw things so clearly, he said, "I can stand on the shoulders of men like Galileo." Good speakers stand to great effect on the shoulders of William Shakespeare, Abraham Lincoln, Winston Churchill, Groucho Marx, even Lee Iacocca.

Using someone's eloquent statement about a subject accomplishes two things: It adds eloquence to your own talk and it endorses whatever you are saying. President Reagan rarely quotes from past speakers who might be expected to agree with him, like Calvin Coolidge. Instead, he often quotes the words of Democrats such as Franklin Roosevelt and John F. Kennedy. The words of these "liberal" presidents not only add eloquence to Reagan's statements but also endorse his more conservative positions by inference.

When you choose quotations to enrich your own talk, be creative. Don't use the same ones you've heard over and over. Go to more modern sources and find a witty or elegant phrase that you can use to support your position. Remember, you're using not only the words but also the person.

All figures of speech have the same purpose—to use a few words to create vivid pictures, touch the emotions, and stay in people's minds. Power language is aptly named; use it well, and people will tend to think you are as powerful as the language you use. As Mae West so aptly put it, "It's not what I say, but how I say it." And what you do as you say it. The next chapter will help you gain power from the nonverbal communication that characterizes you as quickly as anything you say.

Professional Projects: Powerful Language

1. Create a simile or metaphor that describes how you feel when caught in traffic.
2. Think of a complex procedure in your office and devise a simple analogy to help clarify it.
3. Create a title for a presentation on safety using alliteration.

14

Positive Body Language

As I grow older, I pay less attention to what men say; I just watch what they do. —Andrew Carnegie

Although power language can make people notice your words, body language affects your presentation the moment you come into view. Have you ever heard a speaker cover an important topic that was of interest to you, but the style of presentation was so sloppy that you just didn't quite believe what he or she was saying? If your body language is not synchronized with your words, your message will not be clear; people will believe your body language, not your spoken message.

We are a visual society; people start to make judgments based on your body language the moment they see you. No words can convey confidence—or lack of it—as quickly as body language does, and it takes many brilliant words to change poor impressions made by your nonverbal signals. Effective speakers know they must not only master their verbal presentation but also make their nonverbal communication work for them in a positive way.

Albert Mehrabian has said that we are perceived three ways: 55 percent visually, 38 percent vocally, and 7 percent verbally. Audiences are making their hard-to-shake first impressions as you are setting up, waiting to be introduced, and walking to the platform to begin your speech. In short, you are your own best visual aid—or your worst.

Most negative body language is a result of nervousness or lack of preparation. If you are well prepared, the audience will sense it, and your own movements will be far more reassuring than those of the person who doesn't even know how to locate the switch on the overhead projector. And as the chapter on fear noted, a lot of nervousness can be eliminated if you realize audiences *want* to enjoy themselves; meet them halfway with positive instead of distracting body language and the verbal part of your speech will go that much better.

Tackling the Larger Issues

Mastery of body language involves taking control of both the broad aspects of nonverbal communication and the smaller gestures and mannerisms that we often resort to subconsciously. I'll start with the larger points that can add to or detract from your effectiveness:

1. *Preparation.* Besides making you confident and in control, nothing lets your audience know you care like thorough preparation. It's the foundation for building positive body language.

2. *Posture.* Sloppy posture conveys a lack of confidence and possibly a lack of discipline, and it's surprising how many people neglect this crucial aspect of their presentation. Standing erect, balanced between both feet, and with your shoulders back, you convey an alert and enthusiastic manner—even if that's a far cry from how you really feel.

3. *How to approach the platform.* As you wait your turn, maintain a confident but relaxed posture. While you're being introduced, first look just at the introducer and then slowly look over the audience as the host delivers the rest of your (brief) introduction. As you approach the lectern, look as though you would rather be there, about to speak to this particular group, more than any other place in the world. Walk with confidence. There's no particular rule about who you look at as you approach the speaker's platform. It depends on how much space you have to walk across, whether you have to set up your microphone,

whether the audience is applauding, and so on. One approach is to acknowledge your introduction by first looking at the audience, smiling, looking back at the person who introduced you, and then walking toward him or her.

Once you reach the lectern, slow down a little and collect yourself. Always respond to the introduction, but make it brief. You can simply say "thank you so much" and move right into your speech. If you are using a lectern, put your notes as high as possible on the stand, so your eyes won't have to travel long distances. This allows you to maintain greater eye contact with the audience. You should have previously checked the microphone (if you are using one). If you have to adjust it, take the necessary time to do so. Stay calm and in control.

Once your notes and microphone are set, set yourself as well. Balance your weight on both feet; stand up straight with your stomach in. You can place your hands lightly on the lectern but don't lean on it. Don't worry if your knees are knocking. Remember, even if you are a nervous wreck, it doesn't matter as long as your audience doesn't know.

A final note on lecterns: Avoid using them if you don't need them. Lecterns impose distance and elevation; they are barriers between you and the audience. Any book on selling talks about the need to break down barriers between you and your customers, so why create them? Some speakers insist they have to use lecterns in order to feel comfortable. But that's another very good reason *not* to use them, since your audience will just sense that you are ill at ease.

4. *How to use eye contact.* Your eyes are your most important physical feature as a speaker, because they are crucial in establishing rapport. Before you begin to speak, let your eyes sweep the room; look from one side to the other and from front to back. This pause will let your audience know you're relaxed and well prepared. Make eye contact with as many people as you can. Your initial message is that you're glad to be here; your eyes are your first direct contact with the people in your audience—make them support you. Establish rapport with eye contact *before* you begin to speak.

It helps to focus on a friendly face, especially if you feel you have an unfriendly audience. Think of yourself as talking to that open, accepting person; look at him or her as often as you need to.

Most people have a bias toward one side of a room. To discover yours have someone watch you speak. Then when you make your speech, place your feet toward the side of the room you usually miss: You'll naturally turn around and force yourself to face these people. To appear that you are looking at the entire room, divide the room into quadrants and make sure you look into each one. Find a friendly face in each quadrant and focus on that person but not in an obvious fashion—be unpredictable.

5. *Dress.* Comfortable and appropriate are the two key words. Adapt your dress to the people you are addressing; you don't want to dress exactly like them but choose a style similar to theirs. I used to dress quite formally at all times, and as soon as I dropped the formality and dressed stylishly but casually, my ratings improved. When in doubt, dress on the formal side, but try to add some flair; audiences don't want to look at deliberately drab speakers.

Men should stick to the basics—dark suit and white or light-colored shirt for contrast—unless they're speaking at an outdoor picnic where everyone is wearing casual clothes.

Women have more wardrobe options and are more subject to fashion trends. The real key for women is to make sure *you* wear the clothes and not vice versa. Choose clothes that feel comfortable and make you feel at ease. Unless you are known for high fashion or a particular look, it's best to avoid extremes of any sort. Women can wear bright colors: You should not only stand out but also fit in. In front of a conservative audience, you could add some dash by wearing a red scarf with your suit. I know of one woman who stands out—properly—by always wearing a white suit.

Above all, don't wear clothes that need to be adjusted when you stand up or sit down. If you wear a hat, make sure it doesn't hide your face. If you wear jewelry, keep it simple and clank-free. Big bracelets or dangling earrings are taboo, since jewelry can be enormously distracting for an audience.

Women should also try to wear something with a pocket to keep notes and a handkerchief in. Leave your handbag at your seat when you approach the lectern.

6. *How to control your hands.* Novice speakers often ask about what to do with their hands while they're talking. Hands can take care of themselves if you know what *not* to do:

- Don't grip the lectern and hold on for dear life.
- Don't keep your hands in your pockets all the time or folded rigidly across your chest.
- Don't fiddle with your jewelry or props.

Even though your hands suddenly seem to be much bigger than they ever were before, they can be a tremendous asset. There are four ways in which you can use them to communicate ideas better—to emphasize shape, size, number, and direction. Practice your hand gestures until they feel comfortable and natural. Chances are you will feel more relaxed if you have something for your hands to do. If you've got your eyes glued to your notes, your hands will feel like dead weights at the ends of your arms. It's easier to use your hands naturally when you maintain eye contact with the audience.

Practice gestures in front of a mirror—get a feel for what you are doing and what you look like. Strong gestures come from the shoulders, not the elbows. When you break your elbow (try it in front of the mirror, with your hands facing the sky) you'll see what a weak gesture it is.

Use hand gestures carefully, since too many of them are very distracting. When I train people for public speaking

I tell them to keep their arms and hands at their sides if they feel uncomfortable. We discover when we play back the videos of practice sessions that this position doesn't look awkward at all, and in fact comes across quite relaxed. So if you're really uncomfortable about using your hands, just let them rest at your sides.

7. *Your smile.* Unless you are dealing with a life-or-death issue, smile often. It projects warmth and loosens up your facial muscles. Most people look better when they smile, and it makes your audience more comfortable because you appear more natural and confident. A grim-faced speaker isn't going to develop much rapport. Even so, in my public-speaking classes of twenty students, I have to tell at least fifteen of them to smile more often. Try to visualize your audience as warm and friendly, and you will find it easier to smile.

8. *Glasses.* If you wear glasses, you have to deal with how they can appear to the audience. Glasses with heavy rims will hide your face and interfere with eye contact. Half-lens glasses give the unpleasant impression that you're looking down your nose at the audience. The next time you change your glasses, try the kind with large lenses and narrow frames. Stay away from strong tinting or light-sensitive lenses that darken under lighting. Many professional speakers avoid these problems by opting for contact lenses.

You can also use your glasses for effect by taking them off once or twice during the speech, or at the end, when you're getting ready to take questions from the audience. If you've got glasses, use them to give your gestures added impact.

The Fine Points: Gestures and Mannerisms

Your gestures and mannerisms can help you to gain the support and confidence of your audience, or they can make people uncomfortable and even antagonistic. By far

the best way to spot your gestures—both good and bad—
is to videotape yourself practicing or giving your presentation. Replay your speech until you have broken it down
into the series of gestures and mannerisms you rely on.
Here's a list of the most common ones and how they are
perceived:

Defensiveness
Arms crossed on chest
Crossing legs
Fistlike gestures
Pointing index finger
Karate chops

Reflective
Hand-to-face gestures
Head tilted
Stroking chin
Peering over glasses
Taking glasses off—cleaning
Putting earpiece of glasses in mouth
Pipe smoker gestures
Putting hand to bridge of nose

Suspicion
Arms crossed
Sideways glance
Touching or rubbing nose
Rubbing eyes

Openness and Cooperation
Upper body in sprinter's position
Open hands
Sitting on edge of chair
Hand-to-face gestures
Unbuttoned coat
Tilted head

Confidence
Hands behind back
Hands on lapels of coat
Steepled hands

Insecurity and Nervousness
Chewing pen or pencil
Rubbing thumb over thumb
Biting fingernails
Hands in pockets
Elbow bent, closed gestures
Clearing throat
"Whew" sound
Whistling
Smoking cigarettes
Picking or pinching flesh
Fidgeting in chair
Hand covering mouth while speaking
Poor eye contact
Tugging at pants while seated
Jingling money in pockets
Tugging at ear
Perspiring, wringing hands
Playing with hair
Playing with the pointer
Swaying

Frustration
Short breaths
"Tsk" sound
Tightly clenched hands
Fistlike gestures
Pointing index finger
Rubbing hand through hair
Rubbing back of neck

To control your body language, all the points discussed in this chapter have to come together and work for you.

How frustrating it must be for a speaker to deliver a speech with a grand, pressing purpose, only to have the delivery marred by nonverbal mannerisms that alienate the audience. Positive and powerful body language should support your verbal message and help you appear confident, caring, and in control in any situation—whether you are talking to a large audience, your boss, your colleagues, or your family.

Controlled body language that reinforces your strengths as a speaker carries your audience along with you to the point where it gets your message—loud, clear, and compelling. A good way to make that message even more compelling is to add a proper dose of humor, and the next chapter will show you how.

Professional Project: Analyze Your Body Language

Have a colleague videotape your next presentation. Carefully analyze your gestures, mannerisms, smile, posture, stride, and eye contact.

15

Harness the Power of Humor

There are three things which are real—God, human folly, and laughter. The first two are beyond our comprehension, so we must do what we can with the third.
—John Fitzgerald Kennedy

I remember the first joke I ever heard. My father told it frequently, whenever my sister and I got particularly annoying:

> Three elderly women were sitting on the beach in Miami. Two were talking about their children. The first one said, "Ah, my son is a lawyer, makes $250,000 a year, drives a Jaguar, and sends me down here to enjoy the sun for one month every year, and he and my two grandchildren call me up every other week to see how I'm doing." The second woman said, "That's nice, but my son is a plastic surgeon, and makes $500,000 a year. He and his wife have twin Mercedes Benzes, and he sends me here for three months every year and my adoring grandchildren call me every week to see how I'm doing." They turned expectantly to the third woman, who said, "I'm sorry to disappoint you, but I have no children." In unison, the other women said, "What on earth do you do for aggravation?"

This joke, which sticks so relentlessly in my mind, seems to me a model of technique. A joke is a very short short story, one carefully propelled by skillful clues and deliberate miscues. Most jokes are designed to reach a sudden, surprising climax, one that triggers an explosion of laughter.

Why can humor be such an effective device for a public speaker? The most obvious reason is that a good story entertains your listeners. It makes them feel good, makes them more responsive to what you have to say, and convinces them that you're a "regular" person with a good sense of humor. Used with restraint, humor can also make your ideas more memorable, clarify your points, and persuade your listeners.

Restraint is the key word. Go for smiles and chuckles, not belly laughs. You want people to pay attention, not to roll in the aisles (unless, of course, you're a humorist and your main purpose is to entertain). The goal of a powerful speaker's humor is to keep the audience involved.

Making Your Point—Memorably

The best platform humor makes a point, and accomplished speakers favor illustrative humor, rather than jokes that liven things up but serve no real purpose. The best way to use humor effectively is to change the PEP formula—Point, Example, Point—to the PHP formula—Point, Humorous example, Point.

Winston Churchill once advised the Prince of Wales: "Use a pile driver and hit the point once, and then come back and hit it again, and then hit it a third time with a mighty whack." Speakers who use humor to reinforce their points make members of the audience focus in an entertaining way, without making them feel like they are being hit over the head repeatedly with the same point. Whether they remember the joke is not important. What they do remember is the idea that the joke illustrated.

Use Laughter Early in Your Speech

Many speakers use humor at the beginning of their speech, because introductory humor can be a great sales tool. A funny opening sells both the speaker and the speech to the audience. Someone introducing Thomas Edison dwelled at length on the talking machine. When Edison was finally allowed to rise he said, "I thank the gentleman for his kind remarks, though I must insist upon a correction. God invented the talking machine; I invented the first one that can be shut off."

Humor early in the speech works well to establish a rapport, but only if it fits in well with your presentation. Too many speeches start out with humor for humor's sake, and the audience gets put off or sidetracked, instead of involved in your topic.

One of the best places to make a humorous point is in the title of your speech. Every title should make a point, and a little humor can make your audience anticipate the speech to come. You don't need to be matter-of-fact or dull when you can title a speech for telephone salespeople, "Why Am I Still on Hold?" or a speech on public speaking, "If I'm the Speaker, Why Is the Audience Snoring?" One of my favorite titles was for a speech on tax deductions. The accountant who presented the information called his speech, "Everything You've Always Wanted to Know About Charitable Deductions, but Were Too Cheap to Ask."

How to Ease Your Way into Humor

If you're convinced that using humor is a good idea, but you're not sure how to do it, here are a few tips:

■ Don't feel you have to be a stand-up comedian to use humor effectively. Anyone wanting to be perceived as the next Bill Cosby will be frustrated. Come to appreciate your own style rather than comparing yourself to professional comedians.

◼ Be adventurous and give humor a try. Try to add one new humorous story or example every time you speak.

◼ Learning to use humor is not difficult, and it's one investment on which you'll always get a great return. Once you have an understanding of humor, you'll feel more comfortable using it.

◼ Get your creative juices flowing by looking all around you for sources of humor. Politics, news, television shows, current movies, sports, best-selling books, the group you are speaking to, and even the people in it are all potential sources of topical humor.

◼ Read books on humor—anthologies, collections of jokes for speakers, and so on. See what people before you have used in various situations.

◼ Almost every industry has some sort of humorous slant, inside jokes, and vocabulary. I once addressed an insurance group as the "people who knew how to fill out a 5500 C form"—something everyone present could relate to.

◼ The better prepared you are, the more spontaneous you can be. The best way to learn how to come up with something funny on the spur of the moment is to learn how to do this *before* the moment occurs.

◼ If you have a strong comic sense, that's great. But realize that if you can tell a simple story—and I've never met anyone who couldn't—you will get warm chuckles of empathy and recognition, which are just as encouraging for the speaker as laughter.

What to Do if You Don't Get a Laugh

Know when humor just isn't appropriate. Nothing falls flatter than a joke with a negative response or none at all. If you think a joke is appropriate and it just doesn't get a laugh, continue with the rest of your speech. I've also used this recovery when a joke I tell meets with silence: "Well, your chairperson shared that joke with me a little while ago; I guess you can see why she wanted to give it away." Once I heard a speaker add the following when a joke fell flat: "I'm like the famous second-story burglar—except I'm a second-story man. Let me try that one more time." I have also heard speakers point out to their audiences that studies have established a strong correlation between laughter and intelligence, and then pause and wait for the laughter.

The Three Kinds of Humor

Platform speakers tend to use three kinds of humor: original stories from personal experience, borrowed humor, and adapted humor.

Original Stories from Your Personal Experience

Everyone can tell a story, and the stories about you and your foibles are the most humorous. Using humor from your own life brings the people in audience closer to you; they also see and appreciate your ability to poke fun at or make wry comments about yourself. You should always be looking for something to trigger a story. In your little black book for gathering speech material should be a humor section for ideas, stories, and incidents you might be able to use at some later date.

We all have so many stories from our lives, things that are also part of a "common experience." Poking fun at ourselves puts audiences at ease, and once you come up with this sort of angle on yourself, you can reuse whatever characteristic you've chosen. One very successful speaker always makes pointed comments about her height—she's well over six feet tall. I make fun of being short, and the peculiarities I possess as a native New Yorker. Obviously, effective speakers don't dwell on aspects of themselves, but they use those things deftly, to reveal themselves, to establish rapport, and then move on with an amused audience in tow.

Potential material is everywhere. I once was looking for an original story I could use to make a point about how we feel powerless when we're out of control. Then I remembered an exchange my husband and I had the last time he drove me to the airport. We had had our usual "calm" discussion about his driving ability. He thinks it's absolutely smashing; I, on the other hand, am petrified he might be right. After jumping a divider to avoid hitting an oil truck in front of him, he explained to me calmly, while I tried to recover from what felt like a heart attack, that whenever he's in the vulnerable passenger seat, as I was, he feels the same anxiety I was feeling because he's not in control. Looking back, I realized I had a perfect example of a story that could be told humorously.

I have told this story many times, and it always gets a warm chuckle of recognition, because most people can empathize with the situation: They either are backseat drivers or have one in the family. Whatever story you choose to tell, be sure to practice it many times before your speech. Audiences are everywhere; I try out a lot of my new material with cab drivers.

Borrowed Humor

Secondary sources can add wit and authority to any presentation. When you borrow humor from others you often end up borrowing vivid style as well.

Where do you find borrowed humor? The most important source is the printed page—newspapers, magazines, and books. Humor anthologies, *Reader's Digest, Parade* magazine, and your local newspaper are all sources of humor that you can borrow and use in a variety of situations. But never borrow without giving credit, unless you have really changed and adapted an anecdote to fit your own life.

Adapted Humor

Many speakers remodel jokes to fit their situations. A good story can have many lives, and you can edit it to suit many different audiences. The ''light bulb'' jokes that swept the country a few years ago are brief examples of how the punch line of the same joke can vary, depending on who is the target of the humor.

How many Californians does it take to change a light bulb? Four—one to change the bulb and three to share the experience.

How many psychiatrists does it take to change a light bulb? Only one—but the bulb has to *want* to change.

Speakers are always reaching for jokes that allow them to tailor the story to their audience. Here's an example used at a gathering of lawyers, though it could be used for politicians, salespeople, and many other groups:

The Pope and a lawyer went to see Saint Peter in heaven. The lawyer was welcomed first and taken into plush quarters, beautifully decorated and filled with fruit and flowers. The Pope was taken to cramped lodgings—a tiny room with a cot and a single light bulb. He said to Peter, ''I don't want to complain, but why is his room so opulent and mine so plain?'' ''Well,'' said Peter, ''we've had so many popes up here, but this is the first lawyer we've ever had.''

Rules for Selecting the Right Jokes

Choose material that fits your talent and doesn't depend on your weaknesses. If you're not good at foreign accents, stay away from jokes that require one. Most good speakers don't try to act funny or perform stand-up comedy. They look for humor, not comedy. How can you tell the difference? When you read a story or a joke, ask yourself if it's funny on paper. Comedy often relies on a funny character, a funny accent, or some special delivery to put it across. Humor will be funny on paper.

Humor usually reads easily and is also easy to speak. You can use a comfortable rate of speech. It doesn't require a tongue-twisting or machine-gun delivery and doesn't contain a lot of dialogue. When you find a joke with a lot of alternating dialogue, study it carefully to make sure it's not too complex for a comfortable delivery.

Fit your material to your audience. Humor is very subjective, and the same jokes won't be funny to everyone. Some jokes are devices that let the audience laugh at someone. It's essential that you pick the right target. But the platform speaker has an advantage over the nightclub comic: facing an audience with something in common—the same club, the same company, and so on. Shared characteristics make it easier to pick specific targets that your listeners are willing to laugh at.

Members of an audience enjoy laughing at people who they regard as superior in some way, from sweepstakes winners to the president of the United States. Bosses or authority figures are perfect targets, as are government officials and politicians—anyone who is in charge of things. People also like to laugh at anyone who disturbs their peace and self-esteem: in-laws, supervisors, neighbors, competitors.

Although audiences also like to laugh at people they regard as inferior, a speaker can be haunted forever by a public insult that he or she thought was a good joke. If you choose to make fun of groups, do it subtly, as one Baptist minister did. Addressing an outdoor conference on a cloudy day, he said, "Well, the weatherman hasn't done us any big favors today. But this weather isn't bad. . . . It's certainly plenty good enough for Methodists."

There are two important targets to stay away from: sacred cows—people whose accomplishments or reputations make them immune to laughter—and the audience itself. People don't like to laugh at themselves, and audiences are not good sports.

Occasionally, you can get your listeners to laugh at themselves—if you include yourself in the joke. An investment counselor speaking to a group of doctors about stocks and bonds managed this opening: "It's such a pleasure to be able to talk to a bunch of doctors for a change without having to take off my clothes." Sometimes I try to really personalize a presentation by asking ahead of time for the names of three people I can gently pick on during my talk. Clear this beforehand to make sure that no one is offended.

The Best Target of All

You are the best target of your jokes. You not only entertain that way but also win all sorts of extra points with your audience. For one thing, who is going to resent your jokes? You're telling the audience you are a good sport. You win those in your audience over when you use yourself as the target of your jokes, and it's a distinct advantage to have them on your side.

Examples of self-deprecating humor are everywhere. Joan Rivers says she's such a bad housekeeper, she reports a burglary once a year, so the cops can come in and dust for fingerprints. I often refer to myself as someone with a black belt in shopping and tell the story about how my husband didn't report the theft of our joint American Express card—he was hoping the person who stole it would spend less than I do.

The more dignified and prestigious the speaker, the better self-mockery works. Some examples: "Here in the business world I'm chairman of the board. At home I'm chairman of the storm windows." Senator Stephen Douglas once called Abraham Lincoln a two-faced man; Lincoln said: "I leave it to my audience—if I had another face, do you think I would wear this one?"

Here's a lead-in I have heard used (and have adapted myself) that always gets a laugh: The speaker told her audience about studies that have shown people listening to a speech spend 45 percent of their time worrying, 45 percent fantasizing, and 10 percent listening. She then added that she didn't think that was too daunting for her as a speaker; at least she knew her audience was having a good time 45 percent of the time.

Tricks of the Trade

A good storyteller uses a battery of devices to hold you rapt: a smile, a shrug, a cheerful nod, a significant pause, and a rush of energy toward the story's end. But even if you're not a born raconteur, you can carry off a story with aplomb. Follow these rules when practicing telling a joke:

1. Don't oversell the humor to come or promise the audience "this one will have you rolling in the aisles." Better to take the audience by surprise.
2. Don't apologize even before you begin by saying "I'm not much of a comedienne" or "I'm not sure I can tell this right." It's hard for an audience to recover from a negative introduction like that—even if the joke to come is hilarious.
3. Identify only characters, characteristics, or facts that

are going to be essential to the story. If you say, "Sarah Serene, Sunday school teacher," you are cuing your listeners to wait for the point at which her name and occupation pay off. And if you don't, your punch line may be lost in the audience's expectation of something else.

4. Make direct eye contact with your audience during the joke. Look from face to face, and shift your gaze from one part of the room to another. You should have practiced your jokes to the point where you are totally comfortable with them.

5. Have a good time while you're telling your joke—smile and put a bounce in your voice and your step if you move around. If you don't enjoy the story, why should your audience?

6. Speak at a brisk pace and eliminate all but the essential words. A good joke is edited down to its pure essence and doesn't distract the audience with superfluous detail.

7. Stick to simple words that move the story along.

8. Time your humor realistically. Don't tell a three-minute joke in a seven-minute speech.

9. Don't rush the laughter—only inexperienced speakers do this. Enjoy it; don't wait until the laughs die out entirely before proceeding, but don't rush things by cutting them off either.

10. Practice telling the joke in different ways. Always evaluate your reception after a speech and think of ways to shape and improve your humor. Never let it get stale. Sometimes the addition or deletion of a single word makes all the difference.

11. Proceed undiverted to the climax.

12. Deliver a clear, exact punch line.

John F. Kennedy said we must do what we can with humor. Speakers who follow this advice—and who don't overdo the jokes—find humor to be a formidable ally. But it isn't our only one: Visual aids are just as powerful, and the next chapter will show you how to use visual aids to create effective communication.

Professional Project: Simple Ways to Add Humor

You have to present a speech on leadership. Develop two humorous items to include in the speech; use newspapers, magazines, or your own experience as your sources.

16

Visual Aids: When a

Picture Is Worth a

Thousand Words

A picture is indeed worth a thousand words. But it must be a good one. —D. Leeds

We are a visual society; if you want your words to be remembered, give your audience something it can *see*. You have a complex idea to get across: Is there some way to display it visually? People remember 50 percent more of what they see *and* hear than of what they only hear. It's no wonder that visual aids are integral to the majority of speeches and presentations. Visual aids are everywhere today, and this chapter will give you lots of ideas about how to use them—and how not to.

Visual aids have their dark side: As any speaker who has had to come up with some will tell you, they take up a great deal of time and thought; they can take attention away from what you are saying; they are costly; and if anything goes wrong, they can be a catastrophe.

So why use visual aids at all? We use them because a picture really is worth a thousand words. They portray—vividly and instantly—things that would take volumes to explain verbally. They save time, create interest, add variety, and help your audience remember your main points.

A visual aid is any sort of prop you use to support your speech. Charts, graphs, slides, photographs, handouts, and demonstration models are all visual aids. But always remember—you are your own best visual aid. The way you look, walk, use arm motions, and show expression (in other words, your body language) is a key part of your talk.

Visual aids are especially helpful to novice speakers, who may not have the confidence that their own movements and animation will carry the show. Aids also help diffuse any nervous energy by giving you something physical to do. But as with any aspect of your speech, practice is vital. Visual aids that weren't rehearsed will show the lack of preparation, and will accentuate a speaker's lack of experience. If practiced thoroughly, visual aids greatly enhance your professionalism. In fact, I advise my clients and students to use visual aids in all of their presentations.

Put Your Visual Aids to the Test

A good presentation with visual aids is more effective than a good presentation without them, but remember that a visual aid is just that—an aid, not a replacement for part of your speech. To make sure each visual aid you are contemplating will really add to your presentation, ask yourself these two questions:

■ Can I do just as well without it? A visual aid you don't really need creates clutter. Each aid must have a purpose that goes beyond livening up your presentation. Make sure each one you use is related to the subject and adds value to your presentation. Always design visual aids to perform a specific function, and make sure each is self-explanatory and can stand by itself.

■ Is this really a visual aid, or a *verbal* visual? Words printed on a chart are not visual aids; words are what you are there to provide. Sometimes you can find dramatic ways to use words in a visual aid, and they can help the audience identify pictures, but for the most part, use as few words as possible when creating visual aids.

How to Create Visual Aids

A good visual aid springs to life after its creator has followed some basic steps:

1. Go back to the outline of your speech and jot down ideas for visual aids. How could a visual aid help clarify an idea? What kind will work best—chart, model, graph, or illustration? Always design a visual aid to perform a specific function. Use visual aids only where they are needed and make sure they are related to the subject. They should not only liven up your speech but also have a purpose.

2. Write down the essence of the visual aid on a piece of paper and start to work out the way it will look. The paper represents the visual aid; limit yourself to the one or two points you want to emphasize.

3. Sketch out the visual aid itself. You will give this rough sketch to an artist if you're working with one. Whether you are creating your own visual aids or working with a professional artist, always make a rough sketch before you create your final version.

4. Avoid clutter; make your visual aids simple and easy to grasp. If you must combine words and type, strive for a good, balanced layout. Each visual aid should have a title, and should cover no more than three main points. If you have more points to make, create additional visual aids. Limit yourself to no more than six lines on each visual aid; less is definitely best!

If you're using numbers and words on the visual aid, make them large and easy to read; take advantage of the ways graphics can reduce the number of words. Make sure each visual aid emphasizes your main ideas.

5. Use color in three ways: to please the eye, add emphasis, and differentiate one point from another. Even a little bit of color can spruce up a dull visual aid: Underline headings in color and put colored bullets in front of major points. But don't overdo it: A lot of color can lead to confusion. Using too much color is far worse than being overly restrained and using too little.

Color has a psychological impact on most people; we are drawn to the colored portions of advertisements and sales letters. Blue and black are both good for headlines; blue is also good for highlighting and underlining. Green implies *go ahead* and tends to be perceived favorably. Red is an excellent eye-catching accent; however, it is harder to see than the others and implies both *stop* and *losses* (red ink).

So when you work out your rough sketches, use color and practice with it. Try out different colors and get reactions from your friends. In other words, work out the bugs before you finish the visual aids.

Rules to Remember

Bad visual aids—and there are a surprising number of them out there—all share mistakes that the good ones manage to avoid. Here are some tricks of the trade to help you make your visual aids and your presentation look professional:

1. Make all the visual aids consistent but not boring. Titles should be the same size, and type styles should not vary wildly. All charts should use color in the same way: If you use blue bullets for emphasis in one chart, use them in all charts. Never use more than three colors in a visual aid.

2. Keep the visual aid out of sight until you are ready to use it. You want it to support you, not beat you to the punch line.

3. Always talk to the audience, not to the visual aid. Don't let the visual aid become a security blanket; powerful speakers use powerful visual aids, but they also maintain eye contact with the audience.

4. Stand to the side of what you're showing; not in front of it.

5. Don't forget to *stage* the visual aid: Consider the room size, where the audience will be, the easel, power cord, lights, and so on. Clear away visual aids used by other presenters so that you can start fresh. Make sure your visual aids are high enough for people in the back rows to see. If you don't have a stand or an easel, hold the visual aid up yourself, but don't block your face. When you're finished, put all the visual aids aside; don't let them clutter up the platform when you give your concluding remarks.

6. Practice using your visual aids as you practice your whole talk. It's a mistake to practice your speech first and add the visual aids later. Use them as you develop your talk and each time you practice. Make sure they work—and work *for* you.

Darkness Strategy: Avoiding the Pitfalls of Slides

Slides are a double-edged sword: They can effectively dramatize a difficult concept, but they also turn the audience's attention away from *you*, and your visual self is your most effective weapon as a speaker. So if you're going to use slides, they have to be very good indeed for two reasons; to make up for the fact that you're plunging yourself and your audience into darkness and to counter the tendency of most people to lose interest when they hear they're going to see slides. I have seen members of an audience deflate when they hear that slides are part of the presentation, and it's up to you to prove to them— very quickly—that what's coming up won't be disappointing.

Your voice has to be especially lively and dynamic if your presentation takes place in total darkness after a meal. Try to leave some light on; what you lose in slide clarity you more than gain back in audience involvement and alertness.

Despite the drawbacks, slides can work very well and are good visual aids for large audiences. Some situations really call for their use; for example, a surgeon demonstrating a new surgical technique, an engineer showing the ground around a new facility, and a real estate dealer presenting a property would all welcome the ability of slides to present in an instant what would take many words to convey. Sophisticated computer-generated graphics are common in both slide and overhead projector presentations and help speakers convey complicated concepts elegantly.

Slides also give repeat speakers flexibility; they can update their presentation by adding or subtracting slides without changing the entire display.

If you have a good application for slides and are not using them to print words you are already saying, the following rules of thumb will help you produce effective ones:

■ Target what you want the audience to remember, and build your slides around these points.

■ Use only as many slides as you really need. Don't waste the audience's attention by inundating it with superfluous slides.

■ Practice your slide presentation. If you show a slide, make sure you refer to it; don't show a complex slide and continue talking without explaining it. Otherwise, your audience will be trying to figure it out while you're talking about something else.

■ Don't leave a slide on the screen longer than you have to. When you're through talking about it or explaining it, go on to the next one.

■ Prepare the technical aspects carefully. Make sure

ahead of time that your slides are in the correct sequence with the right side up. Number them clearly and make sure your projector and slide carousel are in good condition. Double check everything before you begin: Are the electrical outlets in the right places? Do you have extension cords if you need them?

■ Establish good communication with your listeners before you begin the slide show. Let them know you're the expert, not the slides, and that you really want to be there. Many audiences have sat through boring slide presentations, and you must counterbalance that experience. Show them you are a good presenter who uses slides because you *want* to, not because you have to.

■ Turn the lights off only once. Flicking them on and off is very disorienting for the audience.

■ If something goes wrong with the slides—if you drop the carousel, or they are out of order, or the switches fail, or there is some other emergency—take a five-minute break to fix it; don't try to muddle through the problem. Before you speak, plan in your mind what you will do if you suddenly can't use your slides.

Overhead Projector—The Optimal Tool

The overhead projector is still the most versatile tool for lending visual support to a presentation. And now that computer-generated art can be used on projectors, typewritten pages as visual aids are things of the past—they just aren't interesting enough visually and tend to be crammed with too much information for viewers to absorb. Two of my clients who are very involved in teaching presentation skills—Mobil Oil and Duke Power Company—no longer favor slides. They have joined the ranks of many companies that prefer overhead projectors. Here's why:

- You can produce transparencies easily and inexpensively.
- Transparencies are easy for the audience to read and can be used with large groups. You can project images from a few feet away to more than fifteen feet away.
- You can "interact" with this visual by marking on the transparency during your presentation.
- The projector is easy to carry.
- Duplication is easy and inexpensive.
- You don't have to turn off the lights to use an overhead projector, which lets you maintain eye contact with your audience.
- You can use a white wall instead of a screen if necessary.
- You never have to turn away from your audience.

Keys to good transparencies include limiting yourself to six words per line and using display-size print that is large enough to ensure good visibility. You can also use clip art, preprinted borders, and attention-getting designs. Overlays can provide color for even more interesting visuals. Number your transparencies so that if they are somehow shuffled, you can sort them out easily.

Enhancing Your Delivery

When you add the extra element of an overhead projector, you need to adjust your delivery accordingly. Here are some tips for a smooth presentation:

- Stay in control. If you leave an image on the screen, you're inviting competition, since audience attention is then divided between you and the screen. But you can control attention by turning the projector's switch on and off. For each transparency, you can keep your audience from getting ahead of you by covering specific points with a sheet of paper, and then exposing each point when you're ready to discuss it.

■ Don't annoy the audience by turning the machine on without a transparency on the light table. Learn to transfer smoothly from one transparency to the next, or turn the machine off if you need to pause between transparencies.

■ Don't look at the screen and don't keep pointing at it; when you do either, you lose eye contact with the audience. To emphasize something, point to the transparency with a pointer or pen, and leave it on the transparency. If you are nervous and worried about the pointer shaking, rest it on the projector until you are ready to use it.

■ Decide how you are going to use the projector and place it accordingly. Usually the best place for it is cater-corner, stage right for a right-handed person and stage left for a left-handed person. If you will be writing on the transparencies, you might want the projector directly behind you.

■ Don't weaken your conclusion by starting to pack up your transparencies while you're still speaking. Turn off the machine and leave the transparencies alone. Then move forward slightly to deliver your closing remarks.

Plan for the Unexpected

You can avoid most common problems with overhead projectors through careful preparation and by assuming responsibility for the logistical details:

■ Arrive early to oversee setup procedures.

■ Verify for yourself that everything is ready; don't rely on someone else's word.

■ Locate the on/off switch, since each projector is different, and many have switches in hard-to-find locations. For example, the 3M machines use a bar instead of a switch.

■ Bring an extra light bulb for the projector.

- Carry an extension cord, just in case. Also carry a kit of other supplies—an extra roll of acetates, tape, scissors, tacks, and so on.
- Set up and test equipment.
- Test the lighting with a transparency on the light table.
- Have a contingency plan.

Videos and Films

Videos and films are being used increasingly by firms with sizable production budgets. These media are characterized by high price and a lack of flexibility: Films and videos are not only hard to update inexpensively, but also can't be controlled by the presenter. Since the speaker has to stop the film in order to comment, most film or video presentations are designed for continuous viewing.

These media make up for their drawbacks in sophistication and power. They most closely resemble the television and cinema experiences people are so swayed by, and production can be very slick indeed. When both budget and occasion call for a powerful presentation, these specialized media are particularly effective. If you ever use film or video, get to the site well in advance to check the setup. Nothing messes up a presentation faster than a film that is threaded incorrectly.

Flip Charts

Flip charts are very good for smaller audiences. You can prepare them beforehand, or illustrate them as you go along. They can be actual cardboard displays, or simply an easel and a large pad. Follow these steps as you use flip charts:

- Make the drawings bold and simple.
- Use capital letters and print them.

- Don't talk and write at the same time.
- For drawing, use big, heavy lines. Lightly sketch in complicated designs ahead of time so you can go over them quickly and expertly during the presentation.
- Set up the flip chart ahead of time, but keep it covered until you need it. It should have ring hinges so that you can fold each page all the way back when you're finished with it.
- Don't use red unless you're speaking to a very small group—it's especially difficult to see on flip charts.
- If ink goes through the paper, use every other sheet. It's also easier to flip two pages at a time.
- If you're speaking in a long, narrow room, put the flip chart on a raised platform, or else people in the back of the room will have trouble seeing the bottom of your pages.
- When you're pointing to the chart, and you're standing to the left of it, use your left arm to point. If you use your right arm, you close yourself off from your audience by placing your right arm across your body. If you're right-handed, place the chart to your right.
- Rarely is a flip chart graphically engaging. If you use one, you'll need a lot of energy and an animated delivery.

As with any visual aid, once you've used your flip chart, you need to find a way to get rid of it. You might want to use your flip chart at different times in your talk, so the best thing to do is to have a neutral page after every picture or sequence. This can be a blank page, or one containing a symbol or picture relevant to your whole presentation.

Chalkboards

Chalkboards are also good visual aids for small audiences, if you follow these hints:

- Always check the chalkboard ahead of time to make sure the legs and pegs are stable.
- Have plenty of yellow chalk available, and keep a spare piece in your pocket. Yellow shows up better than white.
- Use damp, not dry, dusters.
- If you use a pointer, don't let it waver around the board. Point at what you want to emphasize, leave the pointer there for a moment, and then take away the pointer.
- Never try to draw or write for more than a few seconds at a time; avoid talking while you're drawing. When you want to explain what you're doing, turn and face the audience before speaking.
- Clear the board as soon as you're finished with what's on it and have moved on to a new topic. Old drawings will distract your audience.

Special Hint for Chalkboards and Flip Charts

To draw straight lines and perfect circles, trace them very faintly in pencil or with chalk before your presentation. Then draw over the lines during your speech; your audience will think you're a latter-day Leonardo da Vinci.

Models and Objects

Models and objects are limited to small groups. Good ones tend to be expensive, costly to duplicate, and often unwieldy. Models require ongoing narration from the speaker to come to life, but this need means that the presenter has flexibility and can change the speech to fit the audience.

As with videos, models work best when the situation really calls for them.

When you pass out objects, samples, handouts, or other materials as visual aids, you lose attention as you do so. Don't introduce vital new points then; rather, use the time to summarize or to describe the object being distributed.

Handouts

Handouts are visual aids the audience can manipulate, so it's important to manage their presentation in a way that keeps you in control. Make it clear what you expect your audience to do with your handouts. Don't give them out without first talking about the ideas they contain, or people will start to read ahead of where you are and you'll lose control.

Save time and confusion and create a polished impression by counting handouts ahead of time. You'll need to know the number of rows and the number of people in each row. Try to be creative with your handouts. Avoid using typed lists, use drawings or other artwork where appropriate. The cardinal rule for visual aids also applies to handouts: They must have a clear purpose and contribute something you could not convey verbally.

Pictures That Tell Your Story

The best visual aids are a kind of shorthand. Charts and illustrations are the visual aids used most commonly and effectively by the creators of slides, transparencies, and flip charts.

Charts are inherently flexible and can show graphs (bar, pie, or line), organizational relationships, cause and effect, and how one event relates to another (flow chart). It's up to your imagination. Whether a diagram, cartoon, map, or original artwork, illustrations make visual aids *visual* and keep them from looking like typed restatements of your speech.

Not Just for Public Speakers

Visual aids—especially flip charts—are helpful for staff meetings and client discussions. They help reinforce your points and make you appear more polished and better prepared. You make an impact because not many people use visual aids in these situations. Just watch everyone perk up the first time you use visual aids at a staff meeting.

A Final Caveat from Murphy

Nowhere does Murphy's Law apply so well as with visual aids: If anything can go wrong, it will. To help you counter this law, I have included a checklist at the end of this chapter. Use it and you'll always be prepared.

Just as Boy Scouts have their motto—"Always be prepared"—a speaker using visual aids must also have a motto—"Always have an alternative plan." And often that alternative plan rests with you. Visual aids can be wonderful devices, but you should never feel you can't deliver a good speech without them; you can. And at all times, just in case, you should be able to.

Vivid, instantaneous, exciting, and colorful are adjectives that can apply to your speech if you use good visual aids. Of course, a master of words can get praise like this for prose alone. But powerful speakers use visual aids to get themselves that much closer to presentation excellence. The next chapter, on stage managing, will show you how to ensure excellence and a smooth show by controlling environmental factors that affect your speech in general and your visual aids in particular.

Professional Projects: Creative Visuals

1. Discuss the visual aids you would use for a humorous and informative presentation on the pitfalls of visual aids. Try to sketch them out, and show how you would make each point.
2. You've been asked to give a three-minute orientation speech to new employees. Describe the visual aids you will use and why you have chosen them.

AUDIOVISUAL CHECKLIST

1. Do my visual aids enhance my presentation? _____

2. Are my visual aids
   Clear? _____
   Simple? _____
   Bold? _____

3. Are they visible to each member of the audience? _____

4. Have I practiced integrating them into my speech at least twice? _____

5. Are they numbered? _____

6. Are they in order? _____

7. Have I accounted for my additional needs, e.g., felt markers or flip charts? _____

8. Do I have an alternative plan? _____

9. Am I comfortable enough to talk to the audience, not to the visual aid? _____

10. Do I have a way to orient the audience to each visual aid and to lead it clearly through each point? _____

11. Am I prepared to explain each step in my own colorful words rather than read verbatim from the visual aid? _____

12. If I am using slides and darkening the room, have I given extra practice to my vocal variety? _____

13. If I am using handouts, have I counted them and fully prepared the logistics of distribution? _____

14. Have I noted on my confidence cards (see chapter 20) when to turn on and turn off each visual aid?

15. Have I carefully timed the distribution of any objects or models to avoid losing the audience's attention? _

16. Have I accounted for both Murphy's Law and O'Toole's Law? (O'Toole's Law is "Murphy was an optimist.") _____

17

Stage Managing: Staying One

Step Ahead of Murphy's Law

If anything can go wrong, it will, and at the worst possible moment.
—Murphy

Stage managing is speech insurance: You may not feel you need it, and you may be right; many speeches go smoothly, and all the unseen details fall into place. But that takes extraordinary luck, and any professional speaker knows not to rely on luck.

A prepared speaker controls the speaking environment; he or she *manages* the setting and the room as if it were an extension of the speech itself. And it is. Speakers depend on their environment to get their points across; if audiences are uncomfortable because the room is stifling, or if there aren't enough seats, the words may be brilliant, but the audience will be counting the minutes until departure time. Do your best to control the environment, and you will control how your audience will receive the words you've worked so hard to shape. Proper stage managing can take the place of a certain amount of talent or confidence. This chapter will touch on everything you should see to before approaching the podium.

It's All in the Details

The more public speaking I do, the more I realize how much can go wrong: On a bad day it's mind boggling, and enough to prompt you to swear off speaking. As a result, proper stage managing seems overwhelming. There are endless details to worry about. Most speakers make the mistake of approaching this task in parts; for example, if they are using visual aids, they may check the equipment carefully but not focus on which seating arrangement is best for showing slides.

Even seasoned professionals can look bad if they have not checked out everything. A well-known media personality and musician was the featured speaker at a recent conference I attended. Although he should have known better, he broke almost every rule of persuasive speaking. His notes were on lightweight onionskin paper, and the lectern was not wide enough to hold both the read and unread sheets, so there was constant juggling and rattling. After he spoke, he brought his messy notes over to the piano with him, and laid them precariously on top. When he hit the climactic chord, the papers cascaded noisily to the floor. Needless to say, he lost the confidence of the audience. A few minutes of thought and planning could have saved the day.

Comprehensive stage managing is best, and that means having a sense of all that you need to check up on. This chapter spells out the many details speakers have to attend to; a thorough checklist is included at the end. Stage managing is an administrative responsibility. A polished, memorable performance, whether in the theater or at a convention, is only the tip of the iceberg. The final, smooth performance is visible, and all the preliminary effort is not, even though the memorable words would not be possible without the stage managing.

George Bernard Shaw once said, "People who get on in this world are the people who get up, look for the circumstances they want, and if they can't find them, make them." A well-managed room is one you set up in the way most advantageous to you. Obviously you won't be able to control or to change all the circumstances that you face, but you can change many of the basic ones speakers often overlook. That's true even if you are part of a symposium or are sandwiched between other managers during a corporate presentation.

What to Watch Out For

Here are the main concerns any speaker needs to address:

Seating and Room Size

Given the purpose of your presentation, what is the best seating arrangement for your audience? Don't be afraid to change the way the chairs were arranged by the person ahead of you; you can call a break to do the reshuffling. If you are specifying seating in advance, be quite clear about what you need.

Seating arrangements also depend on the degree of audience participation. If you are speaking before a large group and limiting participation to a question-and-answer period, *auditorium style,* with its rows facing the speaker, does nicely. *Classroom style* puts three to six people at a long table. *U-shaped styles* that let the audience fan out around the speaker are useful for speakers with small audiences who want to encourage participation. Audiences in U-shaped seating can see both the speaker and each other; the speaker doesn't seem too removed and can walk into the audience.

Find out the size of the room in advance. If you have to choose between one that is slightly too small and one that is slightly too large, choose the small room. Try to get people to sit toward the front, and have someone remove empty chairs from the back, keeping a few free for latecomers.

Speaking Order

Speaking order plays an important role. If you are one of
several speakers on a program, find out when you're slot-
ted to appear. If you can, try to get the opening spot.
You'll be remembered more if you appear first or last, and
first is probably best. If you're last you can sometimes
suffer if other speakers run over their times and the audience becomes restless.

If you *are* speaking last, and you see the program is
running behind schedule, start looking for ways to cut
your speech. It is always better to give a speech that is a
little short than one that is too long. (And your audience
will certainly appreciate you for it.)

Speakers scheduled in the middle of a meeting should
try to get a slot after a break, so they can use the time to
set up. If you can't and have to appear with virtually no
time to set up, try to keep your presentation simple; audiences that have to wait for ten minutes or longer while
you fiddle will lack in goodwill.

If you are the only speaker, you have the most flexibility
and control possible. Arrive as early as you need to to
make sure everything is in place.

The Stage

Many speakers assume they must speak from an elevated
area. Even though I'm just over five feet tall, I try not to
use podiums or lecterns; the height of the former and the
barrier created by the latter put distance between the
speaker and the audience. Remember, power comes from
being close to your audience, not removed from it. But if
you are on a podium or behind a lectern, find out the
height of the podium, whether the lectern has a light, and,
if it does, what size bulb is needed (so you can bring a
spare). Again, if you do have a choice, state your prefer-
ence. I once arrived to give a presentation and found a
huge raised platform—exactly what I did not want—simply

because I had not specified that I wanted to speak from the floor.

Light and Sound

Although the lighting is often handled by someone else, you still need to think about what kind of lighting your presentation will demand and then to make sure the room can accommodate it. Try to have the brightest light available; avoid fluorescent lighting, which can be depressing.

If you are using slides, locate the controls for the room lights. Does the room have many large windows? Will the daylight make your slides too hard to see? Are shades available?

The microphone is another technical detail you confront as you prepare to speak. Make sure you adjust it to the right height for you; the previous speaker may have fiddled with it to match his or her height, and that could leave you stretching or crouching. The best position for most speakers is at chin height, about six inches away, which allows for a comfortable, conversational style.

Once you begin to speak, don't touch the microphone. If it squeals you may be accidentally touching it; take your hand away and it should stop. If you get a loud popping sound from the mike, adjust it so that you are speaking into it at an angle instead of straight on.

As a speaker, you will encounter various microphones. A stationary one lets you keep your hands free. The lavaliere-style mike clips to your jacket or dress; it has a long cord that lets you move around and even walk out into the audience. Many professional speakers travel with their own cordless mike. It's a good choice, but women need to wear a business suit with strong pockets, since part of the apparatus has to be carried on you.

Whatever mike you choose, practice with it first. If you plan on having mikes in the audiences, work with the person who will be circulating, and check out those mikes, too. Always try to get to the room ahead of time, so you can check the lighting, try out all the microphones, and test the sound levels.

Audiovisual Checklist

Every piece of equipment comes with a series of things to be checked:

- Overall condition
- Threading of film
- Switch locations
- Spare bulbs
- Spare cords and cord length
- Order of slides or transparencies
- Condition and location of screen
- Pens and spare sheets for overhead transparencies

Props

Other visual aids have their own vital parts: chalk and erasers for the blackboard, the right number of handouts, an easel for the flip chart. Go through your presentation step by step ahead of time; note everything you need to have. A trash basket? Tape for putting a visual aid on the wall? Who will set up and remove props if you don't? Mentally pack the suitcase you need for a successful speech days in advance.

One prop every speaker needs is some sort of clearly visible timer, to alert you as you go along. It can be your watch—discreetly placed on the inside of your wrist—a clock on a wall you're facing, or someone who will signal when you have five minutes, and then one minute, left.

Spare Parts

The less you leave to chance, the better. Some speakers bring an extra set of their notecards in addition to the obligatory spare bulbs, extensions cords, markers, and so on. The ultimate spare part—one every speaker needs—is a backup plan in case, after all your advance preparation, the slide projector still decides to die as you approach it.

Comfort

A comfortable audience is a receptive one. Professional speakers also attend to the following details, which make for a contented crowd:

- Designating smoking and nonsmoking sections.
- Setting water pitchers and glasses on tables.
- Knowing where the thermostat is and keeping the room at a comfortable temperature. A room will heat up as people fill it; keep the temperature a little on the cool side. Nothing encourages mass sleeping like an over-heated room after lunch.
- Telling people where restrooms and phones are located.

Assistance

In many cases, hotel personnel will be assisting with your presentation. Carry at least three phone numbers of people to call in an emergency: your main hotel contact, a backup person, and a third person or office in case the first two aren't around when you suddenly need them.

Distractions

Few speakers walk into a room perfectly designed for their presentation; more often they encounter distractions that are a function of the room's frequent use. Things to watch out for include:

- *Dirty ashtrays and glasses.* Make sure items used by the group before you have been cleared away. This is true for meetings as well.

■ *Visual aids left up on the walls.* I once arrived to give a presentation in a room where the previous speaker had covered the walls with vivid examples of direct mail campaigns. The schedule was tight, and I didn't have time to remove everything. Now I always find out who is speaking before me and whether they are using visual aids. With the permission of the person running the meeting, I try to schedule a short break to remove materials.

■ *Loud neighbors.* If you are renting a room in a hotel, try to find out who will be in the rooms adjacent to yours. One corporate training session I gave was held in half of a room; a group telling jokes and laughing met in the other half, with only a room divider separating the two groups. It was very distracting. Of course, it's not always possible to control who meets where, but you can at least ask and make your preferences and needs known early on.

Communicate Your Wishes

I always send the organization sponsoring my speech a complete list of my requirements—audiovisual and otherwise. Be as specific as possible; if you think you are spelling out something too much, do it anyway. Never assume. I once asked for a room to be set up "classroom style," because I was conducting a training session. But when I arrived there were no tables for people to write on, even though I had specified they would be necessary. Luckily, I had arrived an hour early and was able to find some tables. Always allow yourself extra time to correct crises.

Careful stage managing is vital before any important meeting or discussion you are involved in. For example, if you are meeting with your boss to discuss your department's strategy for the next year, you will want to time the meeting right and hold it in a place where interruptions and distractions will be minimal.

Check and double-check all details and make copies of

the checklists at the end of this chapter. Don't let the details of stage managing throw you; in reality, knowing you have addressed them makes you appear much more professional and at ease, qualities that you can't help but communicate to your audience. And once you have managed your surroundings, you will be in a much better position to manage the questions your audience sends your way at the end of your presentation.

For those speakers who have to travel to make presentations, I have also included a transportation checklist. The last checklist, the Postprogram Summary, will be of help to professional speakers and those of you who make frequent presentations to the public.

Professional Project: Careful Stage Managing

Develop your own list of details to check and double-check before your next presentation.

STAGE MANAGING CHECKLIST

1. Do I have the phone number of an expert or immediately available helper? _____

2. Have I tested all equipment and visual aids in advance? _____

3. Do I know where all switches are, e.g., the switch for the overhead projector? _____

4. What materials do I need up front?

   Water _____

   Table _____

   Lectern _____

   Chair _____

   Pointer _____

   Markers _____

   Microphone _____

5. Have I checked the requirements for

   Lighting? _____

   Heat? _____

   Air conditioning? _____

6. What equipment am I using? Is everything working and clean? Are there spare parts?

   a. Projector

      Lenses, Attachments _____

      Remote control _____

      Stand _____

      Location of screen _____

      Size of screen _____

  b. Easels (flip charts)

      Type _____

      Clamp _____

      Paper size _____

  c. Chalkboard

      Size _____

      Location _____

      Erasers _____

  d. Video camera and video monitor

      Size _____

      Location _____

      Color _____

      Tape size ($\frac{1}{2}$″ or $\frac{3}{4}$″) _____

  e. Radio recording

      Type _____

      Location _____

  f. Microphone

      Type _____

      Location of audience's microphone(s) _____

7. Have I made arrangements for a nonsmoking section? _____

What about ashtrays? _____

8. Is the room set up exactly as I need it and as I requested, e.g., classroom, theater, U-shape? _____

9. Do audience members have name cards if necessary? _____

10. Is my timer or timepiece clearly visible? _____

11. Have I accounted for breaks? _____

12. Do I know where the restrooms and telephones are? _____

13. Do I need to follow any special protocol? _____

STAGE MANAGING: PERSONAL CHECKLIST

1. Do I have my timer? _____

2. Male and female: Am I zipped, polished? _____

   Female: Do I have an extra pair of stockings? _____

3. Do I have my

   Glasses _____

   Pointer _____

4. Do I have all my accessories?

   Notes _____

   Visuals _____

   Markers _____

   Extra copy of my introduction _____

   Extra items as necessary _____

   Paper clips _____

   Scotch tape _____

   Masking tape _____

   Tape recorder _____(This is a must for self-evaluation.)

5. Is there anything else I know I will need?_____

   _____

TRANSPORTATION CHECKLIST

Travel date_____

Leave office_____

Arrive_____

Depart meeting_____

Means of travel_____

   Ground_____

   Air_____

Hotel confirmation number_____

Car rental number_____

Pickup arrangements_____

   Who_____

   When_____

   Where_____

Directions to facility_____

Shipment of materials and equipment_____

   Method_____

   Date_____

   Name of person to send to_____

Other_____

This form is especially helpful for speakers who give frequent presentations outside of their own organizations.

POSTPROGRAM SUMMARY

Date_____

Contact's name_____

Organization's name_____

Organization (dept.)_____

Organization's address_____

City_____State _____Zip _____

Phone number _____

Type of meeting_____Time _____

Title of my presentation_____

Subtitle_____

Number of people at meeting_____

Type of people_____

Room setup_____

Quality of facility_____

Quality of screen_____

Quality of projector_____

Quality of ventilation_____

Quality of lighting_____

Things to prepare for next time_____

Distance from airport_____Time _____

  Miles _____ Type of transportation_____

Clothes I wore_____

_____

Things for me to do after the program

( ) Read evaluation cards

( ) Sort out follow-up mailing cards

( ) Pick follow-up materials

( ) Sort out my material

( ) Clean out job folder

( ) Save two sets of handouts

( ) Send invoice

( ) _____(miscellaneous)

( ) Write thank-yous to

      _____

      _____

      _____

Key people:

Introduced by_____

Stand-up monitor_____

Other speakers_____

Important people to remember_____

Memorable people_____

Miscellaneous information_____

18

Professional Secrets of

Question-and-Answer Sessions

*More trouble is caused in the world by indiscreet answers
than by indiscreet questions.* —Sydney Harris

A professor at Columbia University's Teachers College
once gave me this humorous but accurate advice: "In every
class you will have a student eager to argue who will ask
a lot of questions. Your first impulse will be to silence that
pupil, but I strongly advise you to think carefully before
doing so—that kid may be the only one listening."

Few speakers would say the question-and-answer period
is the best, or most enjoyable, part of their speech. On the
contrary, even some of the best speakers panic when it's
time for the audience to talk back. They view question-
and-answer periods as barriers looming between the presentation itself and applause and acceptance. But these
sessions are proof your audience is involved and interested. In fact, Bill Lee, chairman of Duke Power
Company, has given speeches just to engage in a question-
and-answer session, because it lets him get his audience
involved.

Those few minutes at the end of a speech let you fill in
gaps, emphasize certain ideas, and clear up misunder-
standings. And the details you go back over and clarify
are chosen by the people you are trying to persuade. It's
participation, not confrontation. The active give-and-take
of a question period yanks your audience out of that passive state known as listening. And you benefit—if you're
prepared.

You Can Finish, But You Cannot Hide

When people come to hear you speak, they expect two things: to hear your presentation and to raise questions about it. They may wish to know more about the subject, or they may want to contest some points. It's true that when you permit questions you risk losing control to the audience, because for that moment the questioner is in the driver's seat. But remember that as the speaker you are automatically in a position of authority and *you* have the advantage. If you handle the questions—and the questioners—well, you extend the power of your speech and leave your audience not only informed but also impressed.

Your objective is to retain as much control for yourself as possible. You can say, "I will take any reasonable question on the information I'm sharing with you." Later on, if you get a difficult question, you can humorously add, "I said any *reasonable* question," and move on. The main drawbacks of the question period are your risk of being exposed to questions you are not prepared for and the danger that questions may come from an unfriendly—or even hostile—member of the audience. But you can virtually eliminate these risks through careful preparation.

Ready Yourself by Preparing

You should practice the question-and-answer session just as you practice the rest of your talk. When you rehearse your speech before friends and family, encourage them to ask questions—tough ones—at the end. Think up hard questions yourself. Get to know your subject so well that you anticipate possible questions, and get ready to answer them. Find your most argumentative colleagues and friends and give them a field day: Chances are they will throw trickier stuff your way than your audience will.

Anticipating questions in advance means you are unlikely to be completely stumped or taken by surprise by a question from the audience. You can't predict and control everything, but when you operate from a position of strength and full preparation, there is nothing wrong with simply answering, "I don't know, but I can find out." Remember that you're in charge of the speech *and* the answers. As Calvin Coolidge put it, "I have never been hurt by anything I didn't say."

You're Still the Leader

People's fears about question-and-answer sessions revolve around these worries:

■ You lose control when you open the floor to questions.
■ You will get a question you are not prepared for.
■ You have to answer whatever question comes along.

These fears vanish if you think of the question-and-answer session as something *you* control. The better your presentation is and the more direction you give the audience concerning questions, the more control you retain. Start by limiting the kinds of questions you have time for: "I will be dealing with questions that pertain to the subject I have covered." Laying the ground rules isn't defensive, it's a sign of organization and leadership: You're still the chosen speaker; you've been leading your audience throughout your speech, and that guidance should continue through the question-and-answer session.

In today's information age, it is impossible to have all the information on a given subject, especially if it's a broad one. As I stated earlier, there is nothing wrong with saying you don't know. But if you set boundaries and guidelines at the outset, you will limit the number of questions that fall outside your area of expertise.

Do you have to answer every question? No. If you feel you do have to catch everything, no matter how off-the-wall, you've already lost your leadership role. Set limits with grace, but set them: There is nothing wrong with telling someone his question isn't covered by your presentation, but that you would be glad to provide him with further information afterward. Your audience will respect you for it.

Banish these preconceptions about questions and you'll find yourself relaxing in spite of yourself. I've seen videotapes of people giving speeches and handling questions afterward; they look more comfortable during the question-and-answer sessions than during the speeches. That's not hard to understand; there is a naturalness to engaging in a dialogue that a speech can't match. Think of your audience as interested, not hostile, and you won't have to worry about what turn out to be good-natured dialogues.

The Right Time For Questions

Because the question period comes at the end of your speech, it's important to do it right and leave the audience with a good impression. Follow these tips to ensure your organization doesn't lapse during this period:

■ Announce at the outset how and when you are going to take questions.

■ Don't give a set amount of time for questions—that way you can stay flexible and if you really run into trouble you can get off the hook by saying, "I'm sorry, we seem to be running out of time."

■ Keep the final minutes of a speech for yourself. They are the prime time; why turn them over to someone else? Whether you're concluding with a summary or some provocative, additional food for thought, prevent a messy ending by asking for questions before you present the real conclusion of your speech. A simple statement like, "I'll be happy to answer any questions you may have, but I would like to hold the final two or three minutes for a summary" will keep you in control.

Those few extra moments at the end will also give you a chance to recover from any irrelevant or awkward questions, and send the members of your audience home with your ideas on their mind, not someone else's.

■ Stay flexible: If you happen to get a great question that ties in perfectly with your speech, by all means use it.

Exceptions to the Rules

Business presentations and training sessions can be far more interactive then speeches, and presenters often don't face a traditional question-and-answer session. In many business presentations (especially informal ones during meetings), the best time for questions can be during the talk, as they come up. This is tricky for speakers, who risk losing their place and momentum. Try this approach only as you become a more experienced speaker. Allow yourself to be interrupted if you have to; if the boss asks a question that fits in, answer it, but as a rule, explain why you would like to hold questions until the end.

There are two general strategies for taking questions in training sessions: You can stop and answer as you go along, or you can take questions after each section of your presentation. The first strategy can get you sidetracked unless you control it carefully; however, the second one doesn't let people ask questions as freely as they can if you take queries as they arise.

Training meetings have a tangible goal: to transfer a skill or technique to the audience. If people don't have questions answered as you go along, you will lose them as their understanding and grasp of the new material slips. As a general rule, ask people to jot questions down as you go along, and stop every twenty minutes or so to take them. If you have someone who just isn't keeping up, don't allow the whole session to drag; you'll alienate the rest of your audience. I tell the person I realize the concept is difficult and that it took me a long time to master it. I then ask him or her to talk with me during the next break.

How to Turn Silence into Questions

What if you ask for questions and nobody responds? This is unusual, unless the speech is on a topic that people are just not emotionally involved in. But if it does happen, it's usually for two reasons: You have answered all potential questions in your speech (pretty unlikely), or your audience feels uncomfortable about asking. Your job is to make them more comfortable. Even if the initial silence simply means no one wants to be first, it can be embarrassing for you. There are many good ways to get out of this spot:

■ Handing out question cards at the beginning of your speech gives people a way of jotting down thoughts as they occur. If you are going to read from these cards, ask for short questions and for people to print clearly. These cards also let people know you really do want questions. They encourage participation in large and formal presentations.

■ Take an information survey (which you have thought about in advance) and ask for a show of hands. The results of a question like, "How many of you feel corporations should do more about day care?" can give you new information to discuss and also gets the audience involved. These impromptu surveys are good icebreakers; they start the ball rolling.

■ Pose your own question by saying, "A question I'm frequently asked that might interest you is . . ." This method gives you more points to cover and buys times for your listeners to think up their own questions. If you ask your own question, make it provocative and of interest to many people, e.g., "How can I handle customer resistance?"

■ Make the first question one you heard from an audience member: "On my way here this evening, your chairman asked me a question I thought would be interesting to everyone.''

■ Deliberately leave out an obvious part of your speech—an omission that will stimulate responses. If you are talking about north, east, and west, but leave out south, someone will be sure to bring it up. You will also find out who is listening. Use this technique carefully, and be sure it works well with your presentation, because if you don't get to the omitted material quickly enough, people will think you are just poorly organized.

■ Arrange with the program chairman to select a member of the audience ahead of time to ask the first question. So if you ask for questions and no one responds, the prearranged ''plant'' will get things going. You don't have to plant the actual question, you just need a willing audience member to help out. But be careful: If the question is very neutral, or if the plant sounds like he or she is reciting a memorized question, you will lose your credibility. As a rule, it's better to choose one of the other methods and opt for spontaneity.

■ If you have saved the conclusion of your speech, you can simply get on with it by saying, ''If there are no questions, let me share this final thought with you.''

Watch Your Manners

The manner in which you accept and answer questions is even more important than what you actually say. You set the tone and atmosphere with your very first answer, and the best way to send the right signal is to have a positive attitude toward all questions. If one person asks a question, it is probably on other people's minds, so when you answer that one person, you're answering everyone.

Since you probably can't decipher the motive underlying a question, it's best to take each one at face value and treat it as a true request for additional information. But your analysis of a question should focus on three things:

1. The content of the question
2. The intent of the question
3. The person asking the question

Never launch into an explanation without fully clarifying the question or being absolutely certain that you understand the question thoroughly. It's all too easy to *think* you understand what someone else is thinking. For example, if someone asks, "How much time should an employee spend on professional development?" a smart speaker would clarify first by asking, "Do you mean during regular working hours?"

Vague questions are traps for both the speaker and the audience. We are so used to them we tend to answer them too quickly. A classic is the inevitable job interview request: "Tell me about yourself." How can we know what the questioner wants? Yet most people plunge in and talk themselves into all sorts of trouble. Just as people try to count to ten before losing their temper, the smart speaker will count to three while asking himself or herself whether the question needs to be clarified?

When you analyze the intent and the person behind the question, remember that argumentative people may be looking for recognition. Give it to them, but don't let them take over. You may lose a few points, but telling them that their question really requires more time and asking, "Can we get together after the meeting?" may be the best way to deal with these people. Long-winded people must be cut off, but you have to do it politely and tactfully. And if you get a real troublemaker who causes a disturbance, chances are your audience will express disapproval and ask him or her to sit down.

Make sure that you treat every question seriously and courteously. The occasional bad apple aside, most people are sincere in their desire for more information. The people in your audience have heard your ideas, and you can be sure they have reacted to them, especially if they are new, difficult, or controversial. Always remember that questions mean the audience is involved with you. Even if the question sounds negative, the questioner may just be expressing some anxiety or doubt. The question may just be the person's way of asking for reassurance. Answer politely and you reassure the whole audience, too.

How to Stay in Control of the Question-and-Answer Period

It's just as important to get your points across in a question-and-answer session as it is during your speech; if you don't, you lose an important opportunity to persuade and lead your audience. You've got three *interdependent* objectives to keep in mind at all times when taking questions. The objectives are hard to separate from each other, and you will stay in control of the question-and-answer session only if you keep all three in mind.

1. Maintain your credibility and control, no matter what happens. Any time you are not believable casts doubt on your entire presentation. And if you get angry or defensive, you lose control. Repeat the question—your audience needs to hear it clearly—and hearing it in your own voice will calm you down.

My definition of assertive is knowing what you want and getting it effectively while you consider the rights of others. The key to success through assertiveness is staying calm, not being defensive, and being courteous. A powerful speaker is one who keeps control of a situation. If you lose that control by losing your temper, you'll never be able to reassert yourself with your audience.

2. Satisfy the questioner. But remember, you don't have to answer the question *fully.* Don't spend too much time with one person. Unfortunately, most of us want to see that look of total approval and acceptance in the eyes of our questioners. But if you spend the time necessary to achieve that look, you will lose the rest of the audience.

Answer in a way that makes your best point in relation to your overall objective, break eye contact, and move on. Saying "Jennifer, you've asked an excellent, complex question. Since we have many other people asking questions, this is the way I can answer it in a limited time" is a polite, honest response that keeps things moving along.

Don't fall into the trap of asking, "Does that fully answer your question?" A dynamic or argumentative questioner will try to hold on to the spotlight and ask for more clarification. Remember there is no law that says you must answer every question fully.

3. Consider the entire audience. You have to let people know you're always considering their time and patience. If you're asked a multiple question such as "How can I cope with not enough staff, not enough space, and a boss who gives me no real authority?" you might say, "You've asked me three very good questions. Because there are other people in the audience with questions, let me answer one and come back to the others if we have time." That way, you partially answer and still keep the audience with you. The audience will respect you for not letting the questioner monopolize the little time you have to spend with them.

If you get a question out of left field, pause and ask, "That's a fine question. Does anyone else here have a similar concern?" If people don't, answer the question briefly and tell the questioner you'll be happy to stay and speak with him or her after the presentation. This technique also works well with hostile questioners.

Keep these three objectives in mind and you will do fine. All revolve around consideration for members of your audience; and the more considerate you are of them, the more they will be on your side.

Never Underestimate the Power of Warmth

Some speakers set a positive tone by complimenting the questioner: "That's a perceptive question" or "That question goes right to the heart of the matter" establishes a warm, receptive atmosphere. Even if the question sounds truly hostile, you can still compliment the questioner: "We can always look to Jack to go straight for the jugular." This tactic is best used occasionally; if you begin every answer with a compliment, you will start to sound insincere.

Save Your Jokes (Or Use Them in Your Speech)

Resist the temptation to be witty or clever when answering questions. Audiences will think you are not taking them seriously, and they will identify—and sympathize—not with you, but with the brave soul who struggled to his or her feet and asked the question you seem to think is silly.

Handling the Hostile Questioner

In general, speakers shouldn't worry that every questioner is out to get them; this is speaker paranoia. But occasionally a genuinely hostile question will get thrown your way. There is only one way to behave if this happens: Be courteous. Never—under any circumstances—become defensive, angry, or snide. If someone deliberately tries to embarrass you, being polite is especially effective. Audiences appreciate fair play and good manners. They will automatically reject the person who is making trouble and be on your side—if you continue to be polite and unruffled.

If you are dealing with a tough subject and expect a hostile audience, asking people to state their names, companies, and so on, can reduce the amount of questions, because many people do not like to volunteer this kind of personal information. This tactic can work at large rallies or in groups where people are not already acquainted.

Being polite doesn't mean you have to be a patsy. If the questioner is out of hand, you can cut him off. If he is especially provocative, you might consider the kind of reply General Hugh Johnson used occasionally: "I'll answer any fair question, but I won't answer a loaded question like this one."

The Fine Points of Mastering Questions

Speakers who handle question-and-answer sessions well have mastered the fine points, too:

■ Give clear directions at the start of the question-and-answer session. Unless you have ground rules already laid, you can't resort to them without sounding like you are dodging questions.

■ Truly listen. Listening well is not a strong suit among many executives, but it's a crucial skill for an effective speaker. The quotation from Epictetus says it best: "God has given us two ears and one mouth—so we may hear twice as much as we speak."

■ Hear from everyone who has a question before returning to someone with a second question. If someone tries to monopolize, say you'll come back to that person after you've heard from other contributors, and make sure you've established this rule at the outset. You can hold off aggressive hand wavers by saying, "Will you hold it a moment, please? I believe this person on my far left is next."

■ Always recognize questions in order. When two or more people hold up their hands at the same time, recognize the first one you see, then mentally note the others and come back to them in order.

■ Don't develop any blind spots as you look for questions. Let your eyes roam over the entire room, including the head table or rostrum.

■ When you're asked a question, always repeat it before answering, since many people in the audience didn't hear it. If necessary, ask for clarification. Repeating or restating the question is one way to clarify it: "As I understand it, you are asking . . ." Don't feel you have to repeat verbatim; you can always restate in a way that gives an impression you want to give. End by thanking the questioner.

■ Always look every questioner straight in the eye. Then answer the question briefly and accurately. Don't wander away from the point. Some questions may tempt you to make a speech in reply. Don't! You have already made your speech.

■ If you don't know the answer, don't bluff your way through it. Your listeners will have more respect for you if you're candid and say you don't know, but you can find out and get back to that person.

■ You may be able to score some important points by asking someone else in the audience to answer. For example, if you are asked a technical question and you know that Jack Jones in the back row is an expert, deflect the question to him: "That's a good question, but it is out of my range. Perhaps Jack can comment." You satisfy your questioner, and win the support of Jack Jones at the same time.

■ Save your conclusion for the end of the question-and-answer session. Only end with someone else if what that person says fully supports your position in a very memorable way. And even if that's the (rare) case, I still like to end the session myself. After all the time and effort you put into preparing your speech, why end on someone else's note?

Rules for Testing Your Answers

There are three tests every answer you give should pass: It should (1) inform, (2) persuade, and (3) tie in with your main purpose and objective. To be informed and persuaded is why your audience is present in the first place; the question-and-answer session is an extension and elaboration of your basic purpose. Make it work for you, and no matter how rough—or how pleasant—your reception is, always sincerely thank the audience for the time and effort they gave to the question-and-answer session and for the ideas they contributed.

Ending with Strength

If you do end your talk with the question-and-answer session, do so before all the questions dwindle away. Try to end with a question from the audience that restates your position. Never keep going until some people are putting on their coats and shuffling up the aisles while one or two last questioners are lingering behind. "Has she finished yet?" one suffering listener asked another as she was departing the auditorium. "Yes," was the answer, "she finished long ago, but just won't stop." Stay in control. End the session yourself by saying, "That's all we have time for today; I want to thank you all for your contributions." Then deliver your conclusion with warmth and confidence. Come forward and mingle with the audience, especially if you have been standing behind a lectern.

If you prepare for questions, take them in stride, treat your audience courteously, and stay in control, the question-and-answer session changes from a worry to an enjoyable opportunity. Make it work for you. The back-and-forth nature of question sessions adds to your credibility: You're not just talking to people, you're engaging them. Enjoy it, and your audience will remember you for it.

Professional Project: Prepare in Advance

You have been asked to give a speech on a highly controversial subject—how to keep drug use out of professional sports. List two tough questions you expect and your answers to them.

19

How to Handle the

Media Like a Pro

It's better to be looked over than overlooked.
—Mae West

Although a question-and-answer session with an audience inspires a fair share of fear, that fear pales when compared with the anxiety caused by facing the media. Yet business speakers are increasingly faced with—and increasingly surprised by—press interest in what they have to say. It's quite possible that the media may want to interview you after you have delivered an important speech. Take these interviews with the press or television reporters seriously. To come off well in an interview, you must prepare as carefully as you did when writing your speech.

Unless you're a celebrity, your personality is likely to have little to do with the media's interest. They're after a news story, and if you want to satisfy them *and* give a good impression, you have to give them that story. Since they are going to write or create a story no matter what you say, you should make it one you want told. And that's where the preparation comes in.

Know Your Objectives Ahead of Time

Before you meet the media, you must decide what your objectives are. What are the main points you want to get across to your interviewers? When you wake up in the morning and read the newspaper, exactly what kind of story about your topic or your company do you want to see?

No matter how well prepared you are, you are not going to get a story that is told entirely from your perspective. And even if your wishes are granted, your story may be presented in a way that alters the public's perception of you in ways you had not planned. Here's an example: A visiting bishop came to a large city to deliver a speech at a banquet. Because he wanted to use some of the same stories at a meeting he was attending the next day, he asked reporters present at the banquet not to print the stories in their accounts of his talk. One newspaper reporter, commenting on the speech, concluded his article by writing: "and the bishop told a lot of stories that cannot be published."

What lesson can you learn from the bishop? If you're talking to the press, make sure you pick out the main points you want to get across and that the interviewer picks them up and isn't sidetracked by a colorful aspect of your talk that you are trying to downplay. For example, if you're being interviewed about a new product, decide ahead of time what product benefits you want to get across. Make those benefits crystal clear in your mind and focus on them throughout your interview.

Don't allow yourself to be sidetracked from your objectives, no matter how dogged the interviewer is. When I was on tour for my book *Smart Questions: A New Strategy for Successful Managers*, one interviewer kept harping on the fact that she thought questions were manipulative tools. Every time she brought up this point of view, I responded by saying, "Let me show you how you can use questions in a positive way. . . ." and would proceed to give her examples. I never fell into the trap of explaining how questions could be manipulative: I kept going back to my objective—to show how questions could be used constructively.

Make sure your points will be of interest to the public at large. Newspapers, television, and radio are public forums, and reporters know their news stories must relate to current public interests.

Preinterview Necessities

Preparation is even more important when facing an interview than it is when you have to give a speech. Although it's possible to toss off an impromptu speech that isn't half-bad, it's extremely difficult to go into an interview unprepared and avoid saying something you will regret later. Here are some of the basics professional spokespeople always attend to before going ''live'':

1. Watch or listen to the shows you're going to appear on. Get to know the interviewer's style, the length of the segments, and the mix of guests.

2. Think of the questions you might face ahead of time—both supportive and antagonistic. Practice your answers to both types.

3. Create a list of appropriate questions and send it, along with whatever supporting materials might be necessary, to the interviewer well ahead of time. And always bring an extra set with you. But be prepared for a session in which the interviewer has not read anything you sent. Not all interviewers will be well prepared, but you should always be.

Fine Points

Certain people make great guests and others just seem to fizzle. The successful ones tend to have learned well the following rules of interviewing:

1. Be enthusiastic. Bring some passion toward your subject to the interview; you're there for a reason, and it's to communicate. Without some passion and conviction on your part, you'll bore the interviewer and the audience as well.

2. Don't give yes or no answers. This is one time when you should not be succinct. Answers need to be amplified for the sake of the interviewer, who is trying to create an interesting show or article. Also, you won't begin to get your objective across if you depend on the interviewer to ask the perfect question; sometimes you have to lead him or her to that question by amplifying on one that went before.

3. Personalize your language; pretend you are speaking to a friend, and avoid technical words or other jargon. Make the interview an extended conversation, not a stiff recitation of facts.

4. Don't bring facts about your competitors or other extraneous information into the conversation. Most interviews are brief, and you should stick to your story as best you can.

5. Use *you*. Many corporate spokespeople are victims of the *we* or *I* syndromes and subject audiences to self-referential tales. You are there because presumably you have information deemed to be of interest to the general public. Involve them by using the word *you* as often as possible.

6. If the interviewer makes an error or says something you feel is incorrect or not true, correct it right away so misconceptions don't linger. If you don't correct a misstatement or charge you feel is untrue, it is tantamount to agreement. So state your disagreement pleasantly and immediately.

7. Always say *something*, no matter how tough the question. The infamous "No comment" is tantamount to a guilty plea.

8. Write a thank-you note afterward. It is a gracious touch most guests ignore and can pave the way to a return visit.

Techniques for Different Media

Three types of media interviews prevail today: television, radio, and print (newspapers and magazines). Each has fine points that go beyond the basics given above.

Television

■ While it may be tempting to look at the camera, face the interviewer at all times.

■ Things happen fast on TV; a half-hour on radio or an hour with a newspaper reporters becomes four minutes on the screen. Try to make your points as quickly as possible, and realize it's an inherently more superficial medium. Don't repeat the question; that only wastes time. Instead, clarify or restate it if you need to, then give a short concise reply.

■ Be sure you get your main point across at least once, no matter how far afield the interviewer tries to lead you.

■ For your clothes, stick with colors that come across well on TV: blue, gray, pale yellow, and beige. Avoid bold patterns and jewelry.

Radio

■ Since your voice has to carry a radio interview and therefore takes on an exaggerated importance, it's a good idea to practice answering your questions into a tape recorder with a friend serving as your interrogator. Play it back and listen to your voice objectively. Do you sound defensive? Are you speaking too fast to be heard clearly? Work on your flaws before airtime.

■ Many radio interviews are now done by phone tie-ins. These interviews can be conducted with you in any location; you just call the station. Be sure to get as many alternate numbers as possible, in case the number you call is busy or not working. Find out what order you should call the numbers in.

■ Try to get on a program that will reach the audience you are trying to reach. For example, if you want to reach a business audience, avoid midday programs, but since many people work at home, it's important to be flexible.

Newspapers and Magazines

■ Read the newspaper or magazine before the interview, to get a feel for the editorial style and readership.

■ Realize that there is no such thing as ''off the record.'' Don't say anything you wouldn't want to see in print, and don't answer any questions you don't understand. Get the reporter to clarify first.

■ Try to arrange an opportunity to meet the reporter beforehand to establish rapport between the two of you.

How to Stay Cool Under Fire

In most situations, the press is satisfied to get the story you want to tell. Sometimes, however, speakers are controversial, and a press conference becomes an opportunity for reporters to open fire. Here are some proven ways to stand your ground if attacked by those in search of a lively story:

■ If your credibility is challenged, don't get shaky or defensive. Stick up for yourself and reiterate or reinforce your expertise and authority.

■ If an interviewer asks you potentially lethal questions, answer in a *positive* manner and defuse the situation.

Recently the president of a new race track was challenged because he was presenting a race with a multimil-lion-dollar purse on the same day as the Preakness. The media were on him like flies, accusing him of using his wealth to ruin the gentlemanly tradition of the sport. The president was a clever and experienced media person. Instead of responding to the notion that he was destroying racing tradition, he talked about all the wonderful things his track was doing for racing and for the public.

■ As any politician will tell you, reporters' questions aren't always traps; you can turn them into opportunities. You don't necessarily have to answer the question that was asked; you can turn the question around. You can even ignore it completely and talk about something else, though you should be prepared for attempts to get you back on track. Whatever you do, don't allow yourself to be baited by the questioner, and don't react by losing your temper: Displays of anger never look good the next day in the morning newspaper.

Listen to the media pros being interviewed on ''Nightline'' or other ''Meet the Press''-type shows. They respond momentarily to the question, then immediately go forward and talk about what *they* want to talk about.

■ If your interviewer says something that you don't agree with, don't let it go by. Correct the impression right away, because silence signals your agreement.

For most people, a media interview is not treacherous. If you are clear about the points you want to get across, and make sure you have a cogent way to say them, you'll be home free.

Professional Project: Handle the Media Like A Pro

You are the spokesperson for a food company in the news recently because it has been accused of adding unhealthy preservatives to its products. You are asked the question, "When will your company show more concern for the public and stop tampering with our food?" How will you answer this question?

20

Delivering with Style

Charm is that extra quality that defies description.
—Alfred Lunt

Enthusiasm Can Make the Difference

My botany professor created a lifelong love of plants in me because he was so enthusiastic about his course from the very first day. On that first morning he literally jumped up and down and said, "Ladies and gentlemen, guess what I have here?" Shivering with excitement he handed us a leaf, saying, "It's a *living thing.*" That kind of attitude is contagious; the best speakers are genuinely excited about their topics. They have passion and aren't afraid to let it show. They know they cannot be neutral or apathetic if their mission is to persuade.

Whether you're facing an audience, active questioners, your boss, or a potential customer, it is your lot that your words tell only part of the story; the rest lies in *how* it's told. No matter how powerful or persuasive your words, your delivery will make or break your speech. Body language makes an initial impression with your audience, but it's your own style of delivery that will continue to shape those impressions. I still remember that high-school botany professor because the way he presented plants was passionate. Look around and listen, and I think you will find it's the passionate speakers who are the powerful ones.

Build on Your Own Strengths

Just as we all have unique ways of walking, dressing, and talking, we also have a unique style of delivery. Videotape yourself giving a speech and look at how you delivered it. Look at four television interviewers with essentially the same job and see the huge differences in style: Oprah Winfrey, Barbara Walters, Phil Donahue, and Dick Cavett—all shape their shows around their personal styles.

The key to developing that style is to recognize your strengths and build on them. If you are a born raconteur, incorporate stories in your speeches. If you keep your friends amused and attentive with lively facial expressions and hand gestures, don't cut them out of your speech. Too much style can be distracting, and some speakers mistake it for substance. I am a very animated speaker and am aware that I sometimes have to tone down my gestures and movements. But for the most part, if you take advantage of your own natural style, it will enhance your relationship with your audience.

Use Enthusiasm Throughout Your Speech

With your opening words, show enthusiasm for both your subject and audience. Let your audience know you are delighted to talk with them.

Real enthusiasm leads to vivid presentations and makes your speech sound fresh to each audience, no matter how many times you have given it before. And you should take advantage of every actor's secret—make each time you speak about something seem like the first time.

Establish a Rapport

Somewhere in the opening of your speech you need to
let your audience know who you are; each speaker does
this in a unique way. Your audience already knows something from your appearance and your introduction, but
you need to let down your guard and reveal something
personal about yourself. It can be in the form of an anecdote, a humorous story, and so on. But it should be
something they can empathize with. President Kennedy
once endeared himself to the French people when he
made a speech in Paris after Mrs. Kennedy had made
quite a splash there. He opened by saying, ''I'm the gentleman who accompanied Mrs. Kennedy to Paris.''

By putting your experience into the context of your
talk, you personalize it; by sharing that experience with
the members of your audience, you interest them in yourself, which will leave them that much more attuned to
your words.

The Four Delivery Methods

Even though your confidence will grow as you get through
your speech, the way it is received will hinge on the
method you use to deliver it. There are four ways to deliver a speech: you can memorize it, read it, give an
impromptu speech, or speak extemporaneously.

Memorization

Delivering a memorized speech is very difficult, and I
don't advise novice speakers to do it. Memorizing puts
too much pressure on you, and unless you're an excep-
tionally fine deliverer, it will *sound* memorized.

Professional speakers sometimes memorize their
speeches because they use the same speech frequently.

Yet for each new audience they make cuts or additions and customize the speech. Only a very fine speaker can do the same speech over and over again and make it seem fresh each time. So unless you're a very proficient actor—or a politician whose every word will be analyzed in tomorrow's newspaper—don't memorize your speech. "He who speaks as though he were reciting," said Quintilian, "forfeits the whole charm of what he has written."

Reading

Reading a speech has similar pitfalls. Unless your writing is superb and you are a true prose stylist, it's usually a mistake to read verbatim. Presidents of the United States are a notable exception, and they tend to have very good writers on staff. I once heard Jane Trahey, a gifted writer, make a keynote speech. Even though she read the speech, she made it work because her remarkable writing carried her delivery.

But most of us are not exceptional writers, and we stiffen up when we have to write something down. Lacking the confidence professional writers exhibit in their prose style, our written language becomes stilted. Compare a newspaper headline to the way you would relay news to a friend. In conversation we tend to be more natural, using shorter sentences, more colorful language, contractions, and slang. We're more informal and more interesting, which is exactly how a speech should be.

Another drawback of reading is that when you read your speech, you're communicating with the text instead of the audience. Novice speakers often believe that if they memorize their speeches by reading them over and over word for word; they'll be able to stand up and deliver the speech verbatim without reading. It's a great idea, but it just doesn't work. And if you practice by reading from a written manuscript, you will become so wedded to the paper that it is virtually impossible to break away from it. You also lose most of the expressiveness and engaging body language that make speeches work in the first place.

If you feel that you must read your speech, begin by talking it into a tape recorder; then type it up and read from that script—at least the speech will then sound like spoken language.

Giving an Impromptu Speech

If you've become known as a speaker, people will sometimes ask you to stand up and give a talk on the spur of the moment. (And this can happen no matter what your status as a speaker is.) Bishop Fulton Sheen went so far as to say, "I never resort to a prepared script. Anyone who does not have it in his head to do thirty minutes of impromptu talk is not entitled to be heard."

Once you've had some experience speaking, you'll probably do a good job with an impromptu speech. Its elements are a condensed version of any prepared speech of general communication. The more you plan, prepare, and polish your formal presentations, the more persuasive you will be in all your communications.

- Know your main point.
- Know your purpose.
- Work in a couple of good examples.
- Try for a memorable conclusion.

If you are known in a certain field, it's always a good idea to have a few brief speeches under your belt that you can deliver impromptu.

Speaking Extemporaneously

If you shouldn't memorize your speech, and you shouldn't read it, and you don't want to speak off the top of your head unless you absolutely have to, what *is* the best kind of delivery? The fourth kind—the extemporaneous speech—is the one that works best for almost every speaker. It means being very well prepared, but not having every word set. From the beginning, practice using notes, but never a typed script. The idea of practicing is not to memorize your speech but to become thoroughly familiar with the expression and flow of ideas. Don't memorize; familiarize. You can also prepare by talking your speech into a tape recorder, using your outline to guide you. Again, talking keeps your speech fresh and helps you avoid the traps of written words.

Rehearse aloud, on your feet, at least six times. Edit your notes after each playback of the tape recorder. The more you rehearse, the better your speech will be. Those who knew Abraham Lincoln well said that the effectiveness of his talks was in direct ratio to the amount of time he spent rehearsing them aloud and on his feet.

Even when speaking extemporaneously, you should memorize certain key elements of your talk:

- The opening
- The transition from the opening that takes you to your first point
- Every important transition that follows
- The conclusion

Memorizing these parts ensures that you will know how to get from point to point and will help you maintain eye contact at all important moments.

When you speak extemporaneously, you incorporate techniques from the other kinds of deliveries. You end up committing certain parts to memory; you occasionally read a note from your notecards; and you may even throw in an off-the-cuff, impromptu remark. Because your delivery style is flexible, the speech can evolve, and you will still be comfortable and in control because you know where you're going and how you're going to get there.

Confidence Cards: Aids to a Smooth Delivery

Many presentations with excellent content are ruined because the speaker uses notes that are either too skimpy or that contain every word of the speech. Properly used, notecards become what I call "confidence cards": They add to a smooth delivery by helping speakers get from one main point to the next. Acting as cues, they contain your speech outline, notes to yourself, stories you will need to tell, key points and phrases, reminders where to use your visual aids—anything and everything that will help you. And they save speakers from their greatest fear: forgetting what they're going to say next.

These cards—whether three by five inches or four by six inches—are easy to hold, don't rattle or shake the way larger papers do, and give an air of professionalism and preparation to your presentation. They are extensions of your own style because they only outline your speech, forcing you to talk in your own words. They also give you something to do with your hands. But you still need to practice your speech many times using the cards, or else you'll tend to go over the time limit or get off the track.

Remember the following key points when using confidence cards:

- Write so that you can see your information easily.
- Make only short, key statements that will trigger your memory.
- Number the cards once you have them all, to protect yourself from chaos if they fall off the lectern. Also, you may need to shorten your speech at the last minute, and you can do that by simply removing a few cards. If they are numbered you know just where you are at all times. To help you make last-minute deci-

sions, try color-coding the ones you can eliminate if you need to.

- Never read from the cards. Glance at your notes and then speak to the audience to retain eye contact.
- Note on the cards which visual aids you are using to develop the key points.

As you go through your notecards in your practice sessions, write little reminders on them: where you want to pause, where you want to smile, and so on. If you have trouble remembering to look around at the whole audience, you can use a card to remind yourself to take in all sides of the room. Confidence cards make excellent security blankets; don't hesitate to rely on them.

The Telling Aspects of the Technical Details

It's not just what you say, it's what you *use* to say it. Visual aids are part of any speaker's style; if they aren't cohesive, they will reflect badly on you. Even the type of microphone you use will affect your delivery. A cordless mike allows you to move around and is a good choice for restless speakers. People whose delivery style is stationary will want a mike they can hold on to. As I said earlier, if you wish to appear intimate, speak softly and close to the mike. How you use the mike can become part of your unique style.

Be Powerful—Be Yourself

A good delivery does justice to the points you've gathered and to the speech you've worked hard to shape. It comes with practice and a lot of planning and from trusting and relying on your individual style. Don't try to adopt someone else's style; your audience will sense something is amiss, and you won't feel comfortable. Be yourself and be enthusiastic, and you will be well on your way to a stylish delivery, ready to use your delivery skills on a daily basis, starting with meetings.

Professional Projects: Focus on Style

1. If someone were to observe you, how would they define your style as a communicator?
2. What are your main strengths as a presenter?
3. Watch different newscasters for a week and define their delivery styles.

21

How to Read a Speech

or Script Effectively,

No Matter Who Wrote It

It is not all books that are as dull as their readers.
—Henry David Thoreau

For every time you may have to give an actual speech, there may be dozens of business situations where you have to *read* key words—your own script or prose inherited from others. Think of the following scenarios:

- Your boss gets a promotion to the London office and leaves you to give his presentation to the executive committee.
- You have a fine speech writer on staff and feel compelled to use her services.
- You must read accurate and precise instructions to your staff in a way that ensures everyone gets the right information simultaneously.
- Reading speeches is the established custom where you work, and trendsetters get nowhere in your company.
- You just don't fully accept all that I've said about the advantages of extemporaneous speaking and simply feel more confident reading from a script.

Think about all the boring speeches you have been forced to listen to. Most scripts that are read are boring, and since my premise is that as a speaker you should *never be boring*, I find it difficult to recommend reading a speech. But for all those times when you have to or want to read, there are steps you can take to make a speech that is read as lively, interesting, and entertaining as one that is given from notes—starting with a concerted effort not to be boring. The lively reading approach isn't easy, but mastering it is well worth the effort.

Reading Doesn't Mean Easy

Don't make the mistake of thinking that having every word in front of you means you can practice less. As an actress I gave many performances without scripts, but I also performed in several productions from visible scripts—where we stood in front of lecterns and *read* our parts. We spent just as much time in rehearsal with productions where we read from scripts as we did with traditional productions where we memorized. It is just as hard to read and be outstanding as it is to memorize and shine.

If you are extraordinarily fortunate and have a speech writer who knows your style and is a good writer, you can get by with one or two practices. But that person is rare, and a speech writer that good is expensive, too. In most cases, you will have to tinker yourself with the words before you.

How to Make the Written Word Interesting and Compelling—Even If It Isn't Yours

The material you need to read can take on many forms; for example, it can be a straight speech or a list of compiled data or regulations. It can be very straightforward and not prone to embellishment: You may have to read a twenty-minute report to the board on safety rules and regulations in your department. Of all the techniques to make your information interesting, practice is the most important. Don't expect to just pick up the information, read it, and bowl over your audience. Reading aloud is a skill in itself.

Beyond sheer practice is belief. You must believe in your message and really want to communicate it to your group. Any audience will be turned off by a reluctant reader who can't wait to finish. At a recent function, I actually heard the speaker, a well-known entertainer say, "I'm going to read my few words and then we can get the hell out of here." Signs alerting your audience to the fact that you would rather be elsewhere don't have to be this overt; an inadvertent sigh can communicate the same message.

Four Easy-to-Follow Steps to Make Any Reading More Interesting

Familiarize Yourself with the Material

The purpose of what you are reading must be totally clear to you. Write out the purpose in simple sentences. This is essential if you are working with a professional writer, and he or she doesn't know your ultimate objective. Your purpose should be prominent in your subconscious and conscious thoughts at all times. It helps you to stay centered and gets your message through.

Read the material several times. Check pronunciations of any difficult words or names. The last name of Hana Mandlikova, the tennis player, could be pronounced MandlIK′ova or MandliKO′va. Which pronunciation is right? It's the job of the speaker to find out.

Separate the whole script into logical parts. Examine each part for its content and intent. Study the words that are being used and the feelings, attitudes, and emotions beneath them. If the writer has used an expression like "deep in the city," is that meant to evoke feelings of excitement and activity, or gloom and despair?

Then pay attention to your verbal transitions. Are they all clear? Are you going to add any physical transitions of your own? Does the script build toward a conclusion, and if so, how is this accomplished? What can you do to complement the writing? (For example, if you were using Julius Caesar's inspiring words, "I came, I saw, I conquered," you might want to raise your arm at the conclusion.)

To increase your overall familiarity with what you are reading, practice as much as you can. Work with the material at least a day before you give your talk, and try to allow a week to prepare in case there is additional information you need.

Personalize Your Message

Once you are familiar with the material, you will need to personalize it, both for yourself and your audience. Make it yours; eliminate any expressions or words that don't sound like you. If you are giving a motivational speech to your department and you seldom use words of more than three syllables, don't call people lackadaisical or ethereal (even if they are). Look for places where you can inject a personal story, or at least start with one. Very often, the best place to personalize will be at the beginning. But don't make the mistake of telling a warm personal story and then totally switching gears into an impersonal read speech. A speech needs to be personalized throughout.

Try to use personal pronouns. Don't say "Employees will resist change if it is not presented in a favorable light." Make sure you say *your* employees or *our* employees or just *you* if you are addressing your employees directly. People listening to you read should also feel as if you are talking to them. Much of the power of our great presidents was directly related to their ability to personalize their speeches. Franklin Delano Roosevelt could personalize so well that on the eve of his death, a young soldier said, "I felt as if he knew me, and I felt as if he liked me." Strive for the same audience reaction.

Wielding Emphasis Well

Using emphasis is the greatest antidote for relieving boredom. Emphasize your important points and de-emphasize what is not crucial. In doing so, you add variety, that delightful and necessary ingredient. Without vocal variety, no matter how potent your speech is on paper, it will sound dull and boring coming out of your mouth.

Great actors and speakers know the secrets of emphasis, which are easy to emulate. One is physical: You can easily make marks telling yourself what to emphasize right on your script; integrating them into your vocal delivery takes listening and practice. You need to become aware of your own vocal patterns so you can make changes in pitch, rhythm, and volume. It takes effort to be on; it's not easy to keep an audience with you. But the people in your audience will love you for not boring them. Even more important, they will listen and learn if you keep their attention. Remember that if you don't have their attention, you're not communicating.

How to Add Emphasis and Meaning to Your Script. First go through your script and mark all the thought/breath groups. These are the places where you'll need to pause to take a breath or to move on to a new idea. Don't follow the written punctuation. Here's an example of a paragraph with written punctuation followed by the same paragraph with thought/breath group punctuation.

No one can understand America with his brains. It is too big, too puzzling. It tempts, and it deceives. But many an illiterate immigrant has felt the true America in his pulses before he ever crossed the Atlantic. The descendant of the Pilgrims still remains ignorant of our national life if he does not respond to its glorious zest, its throbbing energy, its forward urge, its uncomprehending belief in the future, its sense of the fresh and mighty world just beyond to-day's horizon. Whitman's "Pioneers, O Pioneers" is one of the truest of American poems because it beats with the pulse of this onward movement, because it is full of this laughing and conquering fellowship and undefeated faith.

No one can understand America with his brains/ It is too big/ too puzzling/ It tempts/ and it deceives/ But many an illiterate immigrant has felt the true America in his pulses/ before he ever crossed the Atlantic/ The descendant of the Pilgrims still remains ignorant of our national life/ if he does not respond to its glorious zest/ its throbbing energy/ its forward urge/ its uncomprehending belief in the future/ its sense of the fresh and mighty world just beyond to-day's horizon/ Whitman's "Pioneers, O Pioneers" is one of the truest of American poems/ because it beats with the pulse of this onward movement/ because it is full of this laughing and conquering fellowship and undefeated faith/*

Then underline the words that carry meaning, the ones that will require emphasis. You should also de-emphasize all the other words. Here is the same paragraph with word emphasis added:

No one can understand America with his brains/ It is too big/ too puzzling/ It tempts/ and it deceives/ But many an illiterate immigrant has felt the true America in his pulses/ before he ever crossed the Atlantic/ The descendant of the Pilgrims still remains ignorant of our national life/ if he does not respond to its glorious zest/

---

*From Bliss Perry, "The American Mind," in *First Principles of Speech Training*, Elizabeth Avery, Jane Dorsey, and Vera A. Sickels (New York, Appleton-Century-Crofts, Inc., 1928), pp. 216–217.

its <u>throbbing energy</u>/ its <u>forward urge</u>/ its <u>uncompre-</u>
<u>hending belief in the future</u>/ its sense of the <u>fresh and</u>
<u>mighty world just beyond to-day's horizon</u>/ <u>Whitman's</u>
"Pioneers, O Pioneers" is one of the <u>truest</u> of <u>Ameri-</u>
<u>can poems</u>/ because it <u>beats</u> with the <u>pulse</u> of this <u>on-</u>
<u>ward movement</u>/ because it is <u>full</u> of this <u>laughing</u> and
<u>conquering fellowship</u> and <u>undefeated faith</u>/*

In chapter 8 I discussed how to achieve variety through
emphasis in detail, but let's summarize briefly here. To
gain emphasis you can:

Add force or volume
Change your pitch, intonation, and inflection
Vary your pace
Alter your rhythm
Vary your attitude

Listening to yourself is so crucial because you actually
hear yourself change tone, pitch, volume, and so on. Many
scripts that are read are uninteresting because readers follow this pattern: They start a sentence on a high pitch with
great volume and then fade out as the sentence concludes.
Like any pattern, this speaking style soon becomes monotonous. But you can add variety by changing the pattern. Be unpredictable. Pause before an important point;
take off your glasses and look around at your audience.
Reduce your volume before an important point instead of
getting louder. Allow your creativity to emerge. Be dramatic. You may feel silly, but you'll keep your audience
with you. People resent being bored. Whatever you do
to prevent monotony will be secretly—and overtly—
appreciated.

---

*From Bliss Perry, "The American Mind," in *First Principles of Speech
Training*, Elizabeth Avery, Jane Dorsey, and Vera A. Sickles (New York,
Appleton-Century-Crofts, Inc., 1928), pp. 218–219.

Harmonize Your Script and Your Reading

Look at those in your audience and simply *talk* to them:
An effective speech should be an extended conversation.
Even a written speech must sound warm and caring when
read. Use the word *you*. Look for ways to bring the members of your audience into your script, to get them to join
in with you. Instead of phrases like "this next point is . . ."
try "as we move together into this next area. . . ."

Connect with your audience through your words, gestures, eyes, and language. Even though you are behind a
lectern and on a podium, find places in your script where
you can reach out or emphasize a point with gestures. (You
can write these places in the margins as reminders.) Direct
yourself when to pause, look up, or connect with your
eyes. One of the greatest dangers in reading a speech is
that you lose eye contact. That's another reason why practice is so important. Don't allow your eyes to become
glued to the script. Spend extra time looking at your audience.

Since written language and conversational language are
different, adopt a conversational style: Use contractions,
shorter sentences, common words, and the active voice.
You can see the difference yourself between the two pas-
sages below:

> The essential element, noticeably absent, from this
> assembled congregation, was a cohesiveness, which im-
> mediately materialized when the charismatic leader ap-
> proached the platform.

> We weren't working together. We lacked a team spirit.
> But as soon as Tom took over we joined forces and
> rallied behind him. And we're still with him.

One style is dull and removed; the other is vivid simply
because it describes actual people's actions.

Hints for Easier Reading

Since reading a script is a physical activity, here is a checklist of steps that make the physical process easier.

- Use heavy paper—no less than twenty-pound; sixty-pound is better.
- Be sure you have a lectern wide enough for sliding the pages to the other side as you read them. (Do not staple them together.)
- Be sure all the pages are numbered.
- Never end a page in the middle of a sentence or thought group.
- Use only one side of the page.
- Leave a wide margin for directions to yourself.
- Double- or triple-space.
- Use "Orator" or "Advocate" typeface if you are typing your script; both are easy for speakers to read.
- Use a large bold font if you are using a computer's printer, or try regular type on a small sheet and have it enlarged at a copying shop.
- Mark your script for thought/breath groups and emphasis, and put in all your self-directions on the wide right-hand margins.

If you follow these steps and make sure you familiarize, personalize, emphasize, and harmonize, you will become one of those rare speakers who not only present well but make the written word come alive. And the next chapter will show you how to use that ability in meetings, those frequent forums where the written word plays such a key role.

Professional Projects:
Become an Interesting Reader

1. Select an editorial from your local paper and prepare it for oral reading. Practice by recording your reading and then play it back and critique yourself.
2. Find a narrative poem and prepare it for oral reading; then follow the steps for the first project.
3. If you have children, choose a lively bedtime story such as Dr. Seuss's "Sam I Am," and practice reading it with as much vocal variety as possible. Children love repetition, so practice until you are really good with it.

22

Ongoing Advancement: Using

Meetings to Polish Your

Public-Speaking Skills

We are a meeting society—a world made up of small groups that come together to share information, plan, and solve problems. —Michael Doyle and David Straus

People I train always ask me, how can I practice my public speaking more, if I only give a speech every six months? Like any skill, public speaking needs to be practiced often. The answer lies in meetings. Studies have shown that up to 80 percent of executives' time is spent in meetings. Yet many people ignore the chance meetings present to hone their speaking skills and strengthen their reputations as powerful and persuasive speakers. Even small meetings provide important forums to the speaker who knows how to run one properly, since each meeting is an opportunity to give a speech—however brief.

Since most meetings in companies *aren't* run well, meetings have developed a bad reputation as time wasters. This poor impression just makes for more of an opportunity for you; if you can do a good job running meetings, you really stand out.

What to Do Before, During, and After

To run a meeting well, you have to attend to the business of the meeting—before the meeting, during it, and afterward. The "before" stage involves the preparation any good speech demands: What are your objectives, your purpose? What results do you hope for? How does your audience affect those objectives? You'll also need to decide how long the meeting will be, who should be there, and where to hold it. Then send out an agenda you plan to stick to; an advance agenda shows you are organized and capable and plan to lead the meeting well.

During the meeting you use the tools of a speaker's trade: openings, transitions, closings. The meetings people complain about usually lack discipline; people talk on and on to a degree they would never think of if they were speaking before a large audience as part of a formal program. Treat your meeting audience with the same respect and formality you would give to a large audience: Plan ahead; be succinct, vivid, and knowledgeable.

Any successful meeting demands follow-up. Send out a postmeeting summary that includes the title of the meeting, the date, the name of the person who ran it, and who was present. Summarize conclusions the group reached, commitments people made, and what future action the group will take.

The Four Major Types of Meetings

Most meetings fall into one of four categories:

1. Report- and information-oriented
2. Decision making and problem solving
3. Creative and brainstorming
4. Training and skill building

You need to decide which type your meeting will be at the outset. If you can choose the format, consider what you want your audience to come away with. If you have to operate within a set format, you can still shape the outcome by knowing the ins and outs of each meeting type.

1. *Report- and information-oriented.* This kind of meeting requires the most advance preparation. Leadership is very important, since these meetings easily become boring and tend to be filled with too much information. If more than one person will be speaking, try to review the other presentations beforehand, to see if they can be pared down. This preplanning will reflect well on you. Some conferences that overload on information use small discussion groups, which allow people time to digest and sort out information.

The most formally structured of the four types, report- and information-oriented meetings give you plenty of opportunity to shine with an interesting opening, a lively introduction for each speaker, smooth transitions that carry the theme throughout the meeting, and a strong conclusion. What you say and how you say it can leave people thinking they just attended a very well-constructed meeting.

If you are giving a report at one of these meetings rather than leading it, all the rules of persuasive presentations apply. Your report is your chance to stand out from the others. Make it a memorable one.

2. *Decision making and problem solving.* These meetings are tricky because all their aspects demand a display of leadership from the chairperson: where people are sitting, who gets the floor, how long the meeting lasts, and so on. You should make succinct summaries of progress during the meeting. Don't let people get off the track, and watch the time carefully.

Stick to the agenda, which should be clear-cut so people can do valuable thinking beforehand. But don't make the agenda so clear-cut that people are locked into a decision before the meeting even begins. You don't want people coming in with their minds made up. I've experimented with my training sessions; when I ask people to make individual decisions before a meeting, they take twice as long to come up with a consensus as when they arrive with an open mind.

Since this is a "results" meeting, the challenge to you is to move things along and get the group to make the decision or solve the problem. If you can reach that successful point, the results can reflect very well on you.

3. *Creative and brainstorming.* These meetings tend to be free-flowing and minimize your leadership role. But you can still exercise leadership by establishing the right atmosphere, one in which people feel free to come up with new slogans, ways to save money, and so on. Try to be nonjudgmental. I once sat in on a meeting where management wanted to brainstorm ideas for cutting down on staff errors. The first person brave enough to speak up said the company used too many different temporary workers, who weren't familiar with procedures and never had a chance to learn how to do things right. The executive running the meeting cut the staff member off and said aloud, "You are absolutely wrong." Needless to say, no one else contributed after that.

These meetings work best if everyone has a high level of energy. Avoid scheduling them after lunch.

4. *Training and skill building.* Really prepare for these meetings in advance. You'll need to make them long enough so that people will be able to really get involved. Save time for the practicing the members of your audience will need to reinforce what they are learning.

In these meetings, you're really more of a facilitator, so let other people get actively involved. Your audience will learn by doing, not by just viewing and listening. The more they are involved—the more questions they ask, the more give-and-take there is—the better your reputation will be. These gatherings also give you lots of room for powerful summing up; don't be afraid to shine as you impart your final words.

In all four types of meetings, keep the continued attention of your audience by bridging all your topics with transitions and by summarizing frequently.

Here are guidelines for running successful group meetings:

Rules to Meet by
1. Start on time.
2. State the meeting's purpose clearly.
3. Use a title and try to make it—and the meeting—interesting. Call a presentation designed to train people how to fill out new forms "Don't Be Written Off, Write It Down" instead of "Filling Out This Year's Forms."
4. Be positive.
5. Keep the meeting going; guide it along.
6. Remain impartial if people start to bicker with each other. Stress cooperation, not conflict. But if real conflict erupts, bring it out into the open, especially during decision-making and problem-solving meetings.
7. Don't play favorites.
8. Use humor where you can.
9. If someone starts to dominate, it's your responsibility to bring that person under control.
10. Ask direct questions if you need to. Make them clear and nonthreatening and record the answers.
11. Have the person taking minutes read back what people have agreed to do. Discuss decisions, acknowledge differences or problems that surfaced, and sum up what will be done in the future. This person should be an active part of the group, not a secretary.
12. Wind up with a motivational conclusion. This is your chance to show your style and to tie everything together. Don't let people run off early.
13. End on time.

Fine-Tuning the One-On-One Meeting

A quick talk with a colleague or the boss may not seem like a "meeting" but you should treat it like one nonetheless. Even a telephone call puts demands on your ability to organize your thoughts and get your points across. No matter how brief, one-on-one meetings are chances to communicate, and to do it well. Here are some tips:

1. Start on time.
2. Have a clear purpose.
3. Devise a good opening.
4. Be positive.
5. Listen well.
6. Summarize your key points at the end.

How to Introduce Others with Aplomb

Meetings where someone is presenting a report and company get-togethers are just two of the many opportunities executives have to introduce people. These introductions are often done hastily, clumsily, and with something less than grace. Yet they are prime opportunities to make people take notice of your own public-speaking abilities.

Introductions have two purposes: to warm up the audience for the speaker and to help put the speaker at ease, both of which make the speaker's job easier. But the rewards of good introductions go both ways: They provide the introducer with a perfect opportunity to be gracious and charming—in public. Here's a checklist to consult before you deliver your next introduction.

1. Find out what you need to know about the audience. If you can, ask the speaker beforehand what he or she feels would be the most pertinent things to pass on to this audience.
2. Get all the background on the speaker you might need:

special training, positions held, schooling, books or articles published, affiliations, anything particularly relevant to the group being addressed.

3. Construct your introduction just like a miniature speech, complete with an introduction, body, transitions, and a conclusion.

4. Stay away from a joke-filled introduction, unless the speaker is giving a humorous speech or you know the audience well.

5. Try to memorize as much of the opening as you can; it sounds better than if you read it. You want to seem conversational, and reading instills a formality it's your job to displace.

6. Pause long enough to get attention before you begin. Then speak with energy, enthusiasm, and warmth. Remember it's your job to get the audience *interested* in what's to come.

7. Make sure you pronounce the speaker's name correctly.

8. Insert a personal remark about how you met the speaker; it makes him or her seem more accessible to the audience.

9. End with a nice touch like "Please join me in welcoming . . ."; lead the applause. Speakers welcome a warm beginning.

Because meetings are so important I have included a checklist and several forms at the end of this chapter.

Running a meeting automatically puts you in a position of power. Don't wait for the next big speech or presentation; use that position to practice your speaking skills on a weekly—even daily—basis. Recognize that "meetings" occur all the time, whether they are formal and planned or a chance encounter in the hallway. Taking advantage of all your chances to hone your speaking skills is the first step to being your own coach, which is the key to ongoing training and success as a speaker.

Professional Projects: Improve Your Meetings

1. You have been asked to chair a year-end department progress meeting. List the steps you will take to assure a timely and interesting session.
2. Lucky you! You have been chosen to introduce your company president at an employee-orientation program. Write out a powerful introduction, which will make both you and your president look good.

You can use this checklist to evaluate yourself as a meeting leader and to review the presentations of others.

MEETING CHECKLIST

Preparation

1. Were the room and the seating appropriate? _____

   _____

2. Were the visual aids supportive and visible? _____

   _____

3. How were the handouts and support materials handled? _____

   _____

4. Was the agenda distributed in advance? _____

   _____

5. Were the right people there? _____

   _____

6. Were name cards, smoking sections, breaks, and so on accounted for?

   _____

Conducting the Meeting

1. Was the purpose clear? _____

   _____

2. Did I or the facilitator keep the meeting on track? __

   _____

3. Was I or the facilitator in control but not monopoliz-
   ing? _____

   _____

4. How were interruptions and distractions handled? ___

   _____

5. Was maximum involvement and participation encour-
   aged? _____

   _____

6. Was the group and the group process fully utilized? _

   _____

7. Were all the key issues, key commitments, and future
   actions carefully noted by the recorder or minutes-
   taker? _____

   _____

8. Were the presentations interesting, pertinent, and well
   coordinated with the rest of the meeting? _____

   _____

9. Was the timing appropriate to the meeting priorities?

   _____

Concluding the Meeting

1. Were there sufficient summaries? _____

   _____

2. Did the minutes-taker have time to ``feedback'' key commitments? _____

_____

3. If this was a decision-making meeting, was that decision made? Why or why not? _____

_____

4. Were all future actions and assignments clear? _____

_____

5. Was an evaluation form distributed? _____

_____

6. Was there a clear summary and memorable closing remarks? _____

_____

Follow-up

1. Thank-yous sent? _____

_____

2. Any necessary follow-up or commitment? _____

_____

3. Distribution of results (don't let meeting participants be the last to know). _____

_____

4. Announcement of the next meeting. _____

_____

You can get valuable feedback on your meeting style by asking attendees to fill out this form after a meeting.

MEETING EVALUATION FORM

I want to keep improving our meetings. Please take a moment to fill out this form. Thank you for your help.

1. Did you feel adequately prepared for the meeting? __

2. Was the meeting run effectively? _____

3. Could the agenda have been improved? _____

4. Was the group process fully utilized? _____

5. Was the timing appropriate? _____

6. Were you clear on future actions and commitments? _

7. On a scale of one to ten, how would you rate this meeting?

1	2	3	4	5	6	7	8	9	10
Poor			Fair		Good			Excellent	

8. Any other suggestions for improvement? _____

    _____

    _____

TRAINING MEETING EVALUATION FORM

1. The major benefits I derived from this session were:

   _____

   _____

2. The changes I'll make and actions I'll take as a result
   of this session are: _____

   _____

   _____

3. What is your overall evaluation of the workshop
   trainer?

   ( ) Excellent   ( ) Good   ( ) Satisfactory
   ( ) Unsatisfactory

4. What is your overall evaluation of this workshop?

   ( ) Excellent   ( ) Good   ( ) Satisfactory
   ( ) Unsatisfactory

5. What sections of this program were most helpful?
   Why? _____

   _____

   _____

6. What sections were least helpful? Why? _____

   _____

   _____

7. Other suggestions for program improvement. _____

_____

_____

_____

_____

23

How to Be Your Own Coach

'O wud some Pow'r the giftie gie us
To See oursels as others see us!
— Robert Burns

This book has given you specific skills on how to become a more powerful speaker. But it would not be complete without some way to evaluate your progress, which can be a strangely neglected task. I once attended a gathering of professional speakers. A speech trainer was there to critique those who wanted to be evaluated. Only 10 percent of the speakers wanted this kind of feedback, and I was amazed. Getting criticism is the only way to improve as a speaker, and rarely do speakers get the chance to be judged objectively.

Professionals like Luciano Pavarotti, Mikhail Baryshnikov, Martina Navratilova, and Lawrence Taylor wouldn't dream of advancing through the ranks without some sort of equally professional, objective assistance. So they call upon coaches to give them the criticism and support that lead to improvement.

Speakers—especially the occasional, corporate ones—have no such luxury and usually just rely on audience reaction before moving on to the next presentation, which may be months away. But speakers get power only through feedback and criticism. You can be an effective critic for yourself, but only if you go about it constructively. Getting reactions is the first step in becoming your own coach. This chapter will show you how: You can use the forms at the end to evaluate yourself and others; you can give other forms to people so that they can evaluate your performance.

251

Steps to Self-Criticism

In the public-speaking training courses I give, people look
at videotapes of their speeches. When it comes time to
give and get feedback, people are twice as hard on themselves as they are on other course members. When I ask
what they think are their strengths and weaknesses, they
list a long series of weaknesses right off the bat and are
often unsure of any strengths.

For self-criticism to work, you have to be gentle with
yourself and learn from feedback: If people say you were
good, why not believe them? Coaching is criticism, but it
is also developing your confidence by ignoring your inse-
curities and accepting positive comments. You have to be
able to pick out critically the *good* things about your performance, the things you improved since the last speech.
Be gentle with yourself and make self-evaluation an up-
lifting not a negative experience. Here are five ways to
improve:

1. Evaluate yourself. Record every speech you give and
evaluate each one for presentation style, content, voice,
and speech. If you have access to a video camera, you can
also assess your gestures, mannerisms, and overall body
language. Make a list of the things you did well and improved since your last talk, and list the things you still
want to work on. Remember: Be gentle, not brutal.

2. Have someone else evaluate you. It could be a colleague, your boss, or a friend, depending on the situation.
Ask them to be honest and to write down their reactions
as you speak. You can use this technique in rehearsals and
in the actual presentation.

3. Provide evaluation forms after each presentation. Pay
attention to the evaluations, even if they are painful. Listen
to criticism, adapt if it's appropriate, and you will be
stronger the next time around. Once I was told my visual
aids did not look professional; after that I had them done

by a graphic artist and felt much more confident about the entire presentation.

4. Evaluate other speakers. At the end of this chapter is a form listing some of the criteria speakers are judged by. Use it when you attend presentations, and you'll get a much better sense of where you, too, need improving. You'll also become more aware of exactly where and how other speakers score points, since the form breaks down a speech into its parts and makes evaluation a step-by-step process.

5. Practice speaking as often as possible. You don't have to wait for corporate presentations to hone your skills. Join a local Toastmasters chapter; volunteer to give speeches to local groups. The only way to reap the benefits of your coaching and to continue to grow is through more speaking.

Keep practicing at meetings and get evaluations there, too. At the end of each presentation, large or small, ask yourself what you did well and what you need to improve. Before any presentation, single out one or two things you are going to work on and improve, and note them on confidence cards. Practice those improvements over and over; it takes at least seven dry runs before these changes become a comfortable part of your delivery. Realize you only improve a little at a time—it does not happen all at once.

Self-Coaching Objectives

Coaching has one main objective—to improve every time you speak—that you achieve through a series of smaller ones:

- Be kind to yourself. Try to be truly objective about your performance, which means finding both good and bad aspects.
- Don't try to solve too many problems at one time. Don't

concentrate on your weaknesses; pick one or two key things to improve each time.

- Practice self-evaluation regularly; realize it is an ongoing process.
- Don't expect too much.
- Prioritize the things that are really wrong.
- Focus on the six major speaking faults.
- Don't ask your most critical colleagues to criticize you.
- Build yourself up by thinking of how much you have improved.
- Get feedback from other people.
- *Listen* to that feedback; if someone compliments you, believe it. That's how self-confidence and positive energy develop.

The only way to grow as a speaker is to keep coaching yourself. Professionals use coaches because excellence is a process; you learn as you go along, from your experience. Because coaching pinpoints both strengths and weaknesses, professional speakers find coaching to be a very important part of the path to speaking with power.

Professional Projects: Be Your Own Coach

1. Watch a well-known preacher on television and use a speaker evaluation form to critique him or her.
2. Make a five-minute motivational talk at your next staff meeting. Pass out evaluation forms after the presentation.

You learn powerful public speaking by having to speak yourself; you also learn it by listening carefully to others. Use this form when you hear people speak, and it will help you quickly pinpoint common strengths and weaknesses. You can also adapt it for use as a handout after you speak.

OVERALL SPEAKER EVALUATION FORM

1. *The Opening*

   a. Did the speaker appear confident and purposeful before starting to speak?

      _____Yes   _____Needs improvement   _____No

   b. Did the speaker get the audience's attention?

      _____Yes   _____Needs improvement   _____No

   c. Did the speaker direct the audience?

      _____Yes   _____Needs improvement   _____No

   d. Did the speaker reveal himself or herself?

      _____Yes   _____Needs improvement   _____No

2. *Overcoming the Six Major Speaking Faults*

   a. Was the purpose clearly stated?

      _____Yes   _____Needs improvement   _____No

   b. How was the talk organized?_____

      Was there a clear pattern of organization?

      _____Yes   _____Needs improvement   _____No

   c. Were transitions clear?

      _____Yes   _____Needs improvement   _____No

   d. Was there support for the information?

_____Yes   _____Needs improvement   _____No

What support was used? (e.g., stories, analogies)

_____

_____

e.   Was the voice clear, varied, and interesting?

_____Yes   _____Needs improvement   _____No

f.   Did the presentation help solve the audience's problems and meet its needs?

_____Yes   _____Needs improvement   _____No

g.   How did the speaker keep the audience's attention and get the audience involved?

_____

_____

3. *Overall Body Language*

a.   Preparation: Did the speaker make good use of visual aids, notes, room set-up, and so on?

_____Yes   _____Needs improvement   _____No

b.   Were the speaker's gestures, mannerisms, and posture confident?

_____Yes   _____Needs improvement   _____No

c.   Did the speaker smile and make eye contact with the audience?

_____Yes   _____Needs improvement   _____No

4. *Powerful and Persuasive Language*

a.   Did the speaker use colorful examples?

_____Yes   _____Needs improvement   _____No

b. Did the speaker avoid passive language?

_____Yes   _____Needs improvement   _____No

c. Did the speaker use benefit statements and emotional appeals to persuade?

_____Yes   _____Needs improvement   _____No

5. *Visual Aids and Handouts*

a. Were materials well prepared?

_____Yes   _____Needs improvement   _____No

b. Were they visible?

_____Yes   _____Needs improvement   _____No

6. *Handling Questions*

a. Did the speaker maintain control?

_____Yes   _____Needs improvement   _____No

7. *Conclusion*

a. Did the speaker summarize key points?

_____Yes   _____Needs improvement   _____No

b. Was the conclusion strong and memorable?

_____Yes   _____Needs improvement   _____No

8. *Summary*

a. Did the speaker accomplish his or her purpose?

_____Yes   _____Needs improvement   _____No

b. On a scale of one to ten, was the presentation helpful, interesting, and persuasive?

1   2   3   4   5   6   7   8   9   10

No   Somewhat   Yes

9. *Suggestions for improvement*

(If you're evaluating yourself after you speak, you could add the following questions.)

a. How pleased was I with this presentation?

1   2   3   4   5   6   7   8   9   10

Not very   Extremely

b. What can I do to improve?

Six Major Faults

1. _____
   _____

2. _____
   _____

3. _____
   _____

4. _____
   _____

5. _____
   _____

6. _____
   _____

Other Areas

1. _____
   _____

2. _____

_____

3. _____

_____

4. _____

_____

You can use this form with a variety of audiences to get feedback about your presentations. Vary it according to the type of presentation.

SIMPLE EVALUATION FORM

1. How valuable were the ideas, information, and concepts to you?

   1   2   3   4   5   6   7   8   9   10

   Not at all   Slightly   Fairly   Highly

2. How effective was my presentation of the material?

   1   2   3   4   5   6   7   8   9   10

   Not at all   Slightly   Fairly   Highly

3. Compared to other meetings covering a similar subject, how would you rate today's program?

   1   2   3   4   5   6   7   8   9   10

   Poor   Fair   Good   Excellent

4. What idea was most valuable to you? _____

   _____

5. How can I improve? _____

   _____

24

Your Final Source of

Speaking Power

Be skillful in speech, that you may be strong.
—Merikare (2135–2040 B.C.)

The most important thing I can tell you about how to become an outstanding public speaker is this: Analyze your strengths and build on them. If you're lively and energetic, build those qualities into your speech. If you feel comfortable asking questions or taking questions from the audience, do that. If you tend to be serious and more deadpan, look for humor or stories that emphasize or even make fun of that quality. If you're sincere, go with that.

In my speech training courses, if I give a group of ten students an assignment to sell me a pencil, they'll come up with ten entirely different solutions—that's how unique we all are. We're unique in the way we move, use gestures, interpret information, tell stories, and use timing. Even our voices differ. Give a speech and play it back, listening to how *you* sound. Analyze your strengths and look for ways to build on them: They make you unique. Use the PowerSpeak forms to evaluate other speakers and yourself; note what you need to work on.

Once you combine your strengths with an awareness of the six major speaking faults and a devotion to the credo ''Never Be Boring,'' you are ready to build your career and your self-confidence through strong, effective communication.

This book has given you the basics for powerful speaking; the rest is up to you. Good luck, and enjoy yourself as you progress.

The PowerSpeak

189-Point Checklist

Audience Analysis
1. Specify audience's needs and wants.
2. Clarify the theme of the meeting.
3. Indicate the primary interests and fixed needs of the audience.
4. Know the current problems and concerns of each audience.
5. Tailor each speech in some way for each audience.
6. Take into account the backgrounds of members of the audience (e.g. age, religion, education, politics).
7. Assess audience attitude; change talk if necessary.
8. Know the goals of the program chairman and the organization.
9. Ask yourself: "What do I want my audience to know, do, and/or feel?"
10. Find out who will be speaking before you.
11. Find out how much time you will have to speak.

Introduction
12. Have a *short*, interesting, and simple introduction.
13. Build your credibility.
14. Thank the introducer.
15. Give the introducer the script in advance.
16. Practice with the introducer.
17. Tie the introduction into your speech.

Opening

18. Must get attention in the first thirty seconds; use the following techniques:
19.   Rhetorical question.
20.   Audience compliment.
21.   Startling statement.
22.   Startling statistic.
23.   Personal experience.
24.   Biographical information.
25.   Self-disclosure—be vulnerable.
26.   Reference to an occasion.
27.   Reference to a current event.
28.   Quotation.
29.   Declaration of purpose.
30.   Audience challenge.
31.   Historical background.
32.   Subject briefing.
33.   Illustration, comparison, or story.
34.   Create the mood.
35.   Arouse expectations.
36. Let the members of your audience know you are glad to be with them.
37. Build confidence.
38. Share all necessary directions (e.g., when and how you will take questions).
39. Establish leadership role.
40. Relax the audience.
41. Build a bridge from what went before into your presentation.
42. Give support.

Overcoming the Six Major Speaking Faults

43. *Purpose:* A clear focus and purpose sentence.
44. *Organization:*
45.   Strong, logical, and clear.
46.   Logical sequence of ideas.
47.   Easy for audience to follow.
48.   Sequence of points is consistent.

49. Adapt to audience attitude.
50. Adapt to special situations.
51. Clear, definite, and well thought-out transitions.
52. Clear-cut pattern of organization.
53. Frequent summaries.
54. *Information:* Only the necessary material—edit, edit, edit.
55. *Sufficient support:*
56. Make one major point every five minutes.
57. Use sufficient support for the main points; use the following techniques:
58. Explanation.
59. Analogy.
60. Illustration.
61. Statistics.
62. Quotations.
63. Testimony.
64. Restatement.
65. Personal Stories.
66. Use the PEP formula for each main point: *P*oint, *E*xample, *P*oint.
67. *Sufficient vocal variety:*
68. Warm, resonant voice.
69. Firm, supported quality.
70. Build points vocally.
71. Have enough breath to complete each sentence strongly.
72. Stress the most important words and phrases.
73. Shade the less important words and phrases.
74. Thoughts must forge ahead and build.
75. Variety in pitch, force, volume, rate, and rhythm.
76. Correct word and thought emphasis.
77. Vocal and physical energy.
78. Clear articulation.
79. Correct pronunciation.
80. Sharp diction.
81. Full value to all sounds.
82. Do not drop consonants (e.g., gonna, runnin').

83. Avoid "oh", "uh", "OK", and "you know."
84. Sufficient use of the pause.
85. *Persuasive techniques*: Meet the needs of the audience.
86. WIIFM—people in the audience must know what's in it for them.
87. Talk about benefits for each fact.
88. Tie your talk to the emotional needs of the audience.
89. Use the right motivation for each audience.

Handling Questions and Objections
90. Prepare for all possible questions and objections.
91. Have a practice session.
92. Show sufficient knowledge to maintain credibility.
93. Clearly explain how and when you will handle questions.
94. Keep control of the audience and the situation.
95. Use your answers to refocus on the theme or message.
96. Use humor and a light touch where possible.
97. Be nondefensive, not elusive.
98. Satisfy the questioner and the rest of the audience.

Conclusion
99. Must build.
100. Must be strong and dynamic.
101. Tie in to your opening and purpose.

Visual Aids
102. No more than twelve lines per visual—six is preferable.
103. Make sure the lettering is large enough (not typed).
104. Aids must be visible to all.
105. Remove previous speaker's visuals.
106. Use humor if possible.
107. Turn off and/or remove when finished.
108. Practice with visuals.

109. Number all slides and transparencies.
110. Keep some lights on.
111. Label all visuals.
112. Make all visuals consistent.
113. Do they enhance your purpose?
114. Make sure visuals are consistent with your speech and purpose.
115. If you experience mechanical failure, do you have an alternate plan?

Handouts
116. How and when to pass them out.
117. Coordinate with speech.

Delivery
118. Well-prepared.
119. Well-practiced.
120. The illusion of the first time—sounds fresh to *each* audience.
121. Project the audience into the speech or problem.
122. Present a sense of reality and vividness.
123. Establish empathy.
124. Fully memorize the opening and conclusion.
125. Are all transitions clearly written out?
126. Practice with a microphone.
127. Use confidence cards and transition cards; number them.

Use of Humor
128. Use humor whenever possible.
129. Use the right targets.
130. Precise timing.
131. Practice.

Self Disclosure
132. Share yourself with your audience.
133. Laugh at yourself.

134. Show that you care—that you are human, fallible, and vulnerable.

Stage Managing
135. Learn seating arrangements and room size.
136. Check speaking order and your position.
137. Avoid all barriers: podiums, raised platforms, etc.
138. Check light and sound.
139. Set up all props.
140. Designate nonsmoking areas.
141. Set a comfortable temperature.
142. Brightest lighting.
143. Know contact person for emergencies.
144. Avoid distractions—windows, wall decorations, etc.

Presentation Style and Platform Behavior
145. Start strong and establish audience expectations.
146. Be mentally responsive to the audience.
147. Be sincere.
148. Be enthusiastic.
149. Remain poised at all times.
150. Be able to deal with emergencies.

Gestures and Body Language
151. SMILE.
152. Use eye contact with all sections of the audience.
153. Act confident.
154. Posture—firm and secure.
155. Use enough movement to maintain interest.
156. Use strong and appropriate gestures.
157. Make gestures relaxed and comfortable.
158. Have gestures originate from the shoulders, not the elbows.
159. Give your movements a purpose.

Power Language
160. Paint verbal pictures.
161. Use imagery.
162. Use vivid language.
163. Use concise language.
164. Use correct grammar.
165. Use clear and logical thought groups.
166. Use the active voice.
167. Use *you* and *we*—personalize the language.

Handling the Media Like a Pro
168. Clarify objectives.
169. Watch shows and observe the interviewer before the session.
170. Have prepared answers for any expected questions.
171. PRACTICE.

Reading a Speech Effectively
172. Believe in your material.
173. Familiarize.
174. Personalize.
175. Emphasize.
176. Harmonize.

Making a Mark for Yourself in Meetings.
177. Present an agenda.
178. Make your purpose clear.
179. Have a strong opening.
180. Set up an advantageous seating arrangement.
181. Define and carry out your leadership role.
182. End with a powerful conclusion.
183. Follow up.

How to Be Your Own Coach
184. Provide evaluation form for each presentation or meeting.

185. Have two techniques to improve for each presentation.
186. Evaluate and learn from other speakers.
187. *Best advice:* Concentrate on your strengths.
188. Never be boring.
189. Onward and upward.

Bibliography

Adams, James L. *Conceptual Blockbusting: A Guide to Better Ideas.* 2d ed. New York: W. W. Norton & Co., 1979.

Adler, Bill. *The Robert F. Kennedy Wit.* New York: Berkley Publishing Group, 1968.

Allen, Judy. *Picking on Men.* New York: Fawcett Gold Medal, 1985.

Allen, Woody. *Getting Even.* New York: Warner Books, 1972.

—— *Without Feathers.* New York: Warner Books, 1976.

—— *Side Effects.* New York: Ballantine Books, 1981.

Asimov, Isaac. *Isaac Asimov's Treasury of Humor.* Boston: Houghton Mifflin Co., 1971.

Avery, Elizabeth, Jane Dorsey, and Vera A. Sickels. *First Principles of Speech Training.* New York: Appleton-Century-Crofts, Inc., 1928.

Bach, George R., and Herb Goldberg. *Creative Aggression: The Art of Assertive Living.* New York: Avon Books, 1974.

Barnett, Lincoln. *The Treasure of Our Tongue.* New York: A Mentor Book, 1967.

Bartlett, John. *Bartlett's Familiar Quotations.* 15th ed. Boston: Little, Brown & Co., 1980.

Bassindale, Bob. *How Speakers Make People Laugh.* West Nyack, N.Y.: Parker Publishing Co., Inc., 1978.

Becvar, Raphael J. *Skills for Effective Communication.* New York: John Wiley & Sons, Inc., 1974.

Bennett, Millard, and John D. Corrigan. *Successful Communications and Effective Speaking.* West Nyack, N.Y.: Parker Publishing Co., Inc., 1979.

Bettger, Frank. *How I Raised Myself from Failure to Success in Selling*. New York: Cornerstone Library, 1949.

Bittel, Lester R. *What Every Supervisor Should Know*. 3rd ed. New York: McGraw-Hill, 1974.

Blakely, James, Joe Griffith, Robert Henry, and Jeanne Robertson. *How the Platform Professionals Keep 'Em Laughing*. Houston: Rich Publishing Co., 1987.

Boettinger, Henry M. *Moving Mountains or The Art of Letting Others See Things Your Way*. New York: Collier Books, 1969.

Boller, Paul F., Jr. *Presidential Anecdotes*. New York: Penguin Books, 1982.

Bonoma, Thomas V., and Dennis P. Slevin. *Executive Survival Manual: A Program for Managerial Effectiveness*. Boston: CBI Publishing Company, Inc., 1978.

Brande, Dorothea. *Becoming a Writer*. Los Angeles: J. P. Tarcher, Inc., 1981.

Brandreth, Gyles. *The Biggest Tongue Twister Book in the World*. New York: Sterling Publishing Co., Inc., 1981.

Braude, Jacob M. *Braude's Treasury of Wit & Humor*. Englewood Cliffs, N.J.: Prentice-Hall, Inc., 1964.

———. *Braude's Handbook of Stories for Toastmasters and Speakers*. Englewood Cliffs, N.J.: Prentice-Hall, Inc., 1975.

Bremer, Roslyn. *How to Write a Speech—One That Talks*. New York: Kodama Arts, 1980.

Breslin, Mark, Eve Drobot, and Larry Horowitz. *Zen and Now: The Baby Boomer's Guide to Middle Life*. Toronto, Ont.: Somerville House Books Ltd., 1985.

Brill, Laura. *Business Writing Quick and Easy*. New York: American Management Association, 1981.

Bristol, Claude M. *The Magic of Believing*. New York: Pocket Books, 1975.

Brooks, Mel, and Carl Reiner. *The 2,000 Year Old Man*. New York: Warner Books, 1981.

Brown, Ronald. *From Selling to Managing*. New York: Amacom, 1968.

Campbell, David. *If I'm in Charge Here Why Is Everybody Laughing?* Allen, Tex.: Argus Communications, 1980.

——. *Take the Road to Creativity and Get Off Your Dead End.* Allen, Tex.: Argus Communications, 1980.

Carlile, Clark S. *Project Text for Public Speaking.* New York: Harper & Brothers, 1953.

Carnegie, Dale. *How to Develop Self-Confidence and Influence People by Public Speaking.* New York: Pocket Books, 1956.

Carroll, Donald. *Why Didn't I Say That? The Art of Verbal Self-Defense.* New York: Franklin Watts, 1980.

Cohen, Herb. *You Can Negotiate Anything: How to Get What You Want.* Secaucus, N.J.: Lyle Stuart, 1980.

Cooper, Ken. *Nonverbal Communication for Business Success.* New York: American Management Association, 1979.

Copeland, Lewis, and Faye Copeland, eds. *10,000 Jokes, Toasts and Stories.* Garden City, N.Y.: Doubleday & Co., Inc., 1965.

Crosbie, John S. *Crosbie's Dictionary of Puns.* New York: Harmony Books, 1977.

——. *Crosbie's Dictionary of Riddles.* New York: Harmony Books, 1980.

Culbert, Clifford J., and Richard Conrad. *How to Communicate and Succeed.* New York: Vantage Press, 1970.

Dane, Les. *Surefire Sales Closing Techniques.* West Nyack, N.Y.: Parker Publishing Co., Inc., 1971.

Day, Mahlon. *New York Street Cries in Rhyme.* New York: Dover Publications, 1977.

De Bono, Edward. *Lateral Thinking: Creativity Step by Step.* New York: Harper & Row Publishers, 1970.

Dickson, Paul. *The Official Rules.* New York: Dell Publishing Co., Inc., 1978.

Dineen, Jacqueline. *Remembering Made Easy.* Wellingborough, U.K.: Thomson Publishers Ltd., 1977.

——. *Talking Your Way to Success.* Wellingborough, U.K.: Thomson Publishers Ltd., 1977.

Dowdall, Mike, and Pat Welch. *Humans at Work*. New York: Simon & Schuster, Inc., 1986.

Doyle, Michael, and David Strauss. *The New Interaction Method: How to Make Meetings Work*. Chicago: Playboy Press, 1976.

Dychtwald, Ken. *Body-Mind*. New York: Jove, 1978.

Eisen, Jeffrey, and Pat Farley. *Powertalk! How to Speak It. Think It. and Use It*. New York: Cornerstone Library, 1984.

Elgin Haden, Suzette. *The Gentle Art of Verbal Self-Defense*. Englewood Cliffs, N.J.: Prentice-Hall, Inc., 1980.

The English Language Arts. New York: Appleton-Century-Crofts, Inc., 1952.

Fast, Julius. *Body Language*. New York: Pocket Books, 1971.

Fast, Julius, and Barbara Fast. *Talking Between the Lines*. New York: Viking Press, 1979.

Fechtner, Leopold. *5,000 One and Two Liners for Any and Every Occasion*. West Nyack, N.Y.: Parker Publishing Co., Inc., 1973.

Fensterheim, Herbert. *Don't Say Yes When You Want to Say No*. New York: Dell Publishing Co., Inc., 1975.

Ferguson von Hesse, Elizabeth. *So to Speak: A Practical Training Course for Developing a Beautiful Speaking Voice*. Philadelphia: J. B. Lippincott Co., 1959.

Fischer, Martin. *Gracian's Manual*. Springfield, Ill.: Charles C. Thomas Publishers, 1945.

Fish, Jim, and Robert Barron. *The Official MBA Handbook of Great Business Quotations*. New York: Simon & Schuster, Inc., 1984.

———. *The ABC of Style: A Guide to Plain English*. New York: Harper & Row Publishers, 1964.

Flesch, Rudolf. *The Art of Readable Writing*. New York: Macmillan Publishing Co., Inc., 1962.

Fletcher, Winston. *Meetings, Meetings: How to Manipu-*

late Them and Make Them More Fun. London: Michael Joseph, 1983.

Forley, Maurice. *A Practical Guide to Public Speaking.* North Hollywood, Calif.: Wilshire Book Co., 1970.

Gawain, Shakti. *Creative Visualization.* New York: Bantam New Age, 1982.

Gaylin, William. *Feelings.* New York: Ballantine Books, 1982.

Gilbert, Michael A. *How to Win an Argument.* New York: McGraw-Hill, 1979.

Gordon, Thomas. *Leader Effective Training.* New York: Bantam Books, 1977.

Graves, Robert, and Alan Hodge. *The Reader over Your Shoulder: A Handbook for Writers of English Prose.* New York: Random House, Inc., 1979.

Gray, Giles, and Claude Wise. *The Bases of Speech.* New York: Harper & Brothers, 1946.

Gray, James, Jr. *The Winning Image.* New York: Amacom, 1982.

Greenburg, Daniel, and Marcia Jacobs. *How to Make Yourself Miserable.* New York: Random House, Inc., 1966.

Gren, Jack. *The Executive's Guide to Successful Speechmaking.* New York: Pilot Books, 1969.

Hahn, George N. *The 36 Biggest Mistakes Salesmen Make and How to Correct Them.* Englewood Cliffs, N.J.: Prentice-Hall, Inc., 1963.

Hall, Edward T. *The Hidden Dimension.* Garden City. N.Y.: Anchor, 1969.

Hall, Rich, and friends. *More Sniglets.* New York: Collier Books, 1985.

Halliwell, Leslie. *The Filmgoer's Book of Quotes.* New York: New American Library, 1975.

Hanan, Mack. *Life-Styled Marketing.* Rev. ed. New York: American Management Association, 1972.

Hanan, Mack, Howard Berrian, and James Cribbin. *Sales Negotiation Strategies.* New York: Amacom, 1977.

Hanan, Mack, Howard Berrian, James Cribbin, and Jack Donis. *Take-Charge Sales Management.* New York: Amacom, 1976.

Harrison, Allen F., and Robert M. Bramson. *The Art of Thinking: Strategies for Asking Questions, Making Decisions, and Solving Problems.* New York: Berkley Publishing Group, 1982.

Hart, Lois B. *Learning from Conflict: A Handbook for Trainers and Group Leaders.* Reading, Mass.: Addison-Wesley Publishing Co., 1981.

Hegarty, Edward. *How to Talk Your Way to the Top.* West Nyack, N.Y.: Parker Publishing Co. Inc., 1973.

Hennig, Margaret, and Anne Jardim. *The Managerial Woman.* Garden City, N.Y.: Anchor Press/Doubleday, 1977.

Herman, Lewis, and Marguerite Shalett Herman. *Foreign Dialects.* New York: Theatre Arts Books, 1943.

———. *American Dialects.* New York: Theatre Arts Books, 1947.

Herndon, Booten, ed. *The Humor of J.F.K.* Greenwich, Conn.: Fawcett Gold Medal, 1964.

Higginson, Margaret V., and Thomas L. Quick. *The Ambitious Woman's Guide to a Successful Career.* New York: American Management Association, 1975.

Hill, Napolean, and W. Clement Stone. *Success Through a Positive Mental Attitude.* New York: Pocket Books, 1977.

Humes, James C. *Podium Humor.* New York: Perennial Library, 1975.

———. *Speaker's Treasury of Anecdotes About the Famous.* New York: Barnes & Noble Books, 1985.

Huskey, Ken W. *Spokesperson.* Palm Springs, Calif.: K. W. Huskey Assoc., 1980.

Jay, Antony. *The New Oratory.* New York: American Management Association, 1971.

Jesen, Dana O., John Francis McDermott, and Kendall B. Taft. *The Technique of Composition.* New York: Rinehart & Co., 1946.

Jones, Daniel. *Everyman's English Pronouncing Dictionary.* Edited by A. C. Gimson. New York: E. P. Dutton & Co., Inc., 1967.

Kennedy, Marilyn Moats, *Office Politics—Seizing Power, Wielding Clout.* New York: Warner Books, 1981.

Kenyon, John S. and Thomas A. Knott. *A Pronouncing Dictionary of American English.* Springfield, Mass.: G. & C. Merriam Co., 1953.

Klein, Ted, and Fred Danzig. *How to Be Heard.* New York: Macmillan Publishing Co., Inc., 1974.

Kotter, John P. *Power in Management: How to Understand, Acquire, and Use It.* New York: American Management Association, 1979.

Laird, Charlton. *The Miracle of Language.* New York: Fawcett Publications, Inc., 1957.

Lazarus, Arnold, and Fay Allen. *I Can if I Want To.* New York: Warner Books, 1975.

Lee, Irving. *The Language of Wisdom and Folly.* New York: Harper & Brothers, 1949.

Leech, Thomas. *How to Prepare, Stage, and Deliver Winning Presentations.* New York: Amacom, 1982.

Lewis, Norman. *Better English.* New York: Dell Publishing Co., Inc., 1961.

———. *Correct Spelling Made Easy.* New York: Dell Publishing Co., Inc., 1963.

Leiberman, Gerald F. *3,500 Good Jokes for Speakers.* Garden City, N.Y.: Doubleday & Co., Inc., 1975.

Ling, Mona. *How to Increase Sales and Put Yourself Across by Telephone.* Englewood Cliffs, N.J.: Prentice-Hall, Inc., 1963.

Lorayne, Harry. *Remembering People—The Key to Success.* Briarcliff Manor, N.Y.: Stein & Day, 1975.

Lumsden, George. *Impact Managment: Personal Power Strategies for Success.* New York: American Management Association, 1979.

Lund, Philip R. *Compelling Spelling.* New York: American Management Association, 1978.

Mager, N. H., S. K. Mager, and P. S. Mager, eds, and comps. *Power Writing, Power Speaking.* New York: William Morrow & Co., 1978.

Mager, Robert F., and Peter Pipe. *Analyzing Performance Problems, or, You Really Oughta Wanna.* Belmont, Calif.: Fearon Publishers, 1970.

Mance, Kenneth G., and James H. McBurney. *Discussion in Human Affairs.* New York: Harper & Brothers, 1959.

Mandino, Og. *The Greatest Salesman in the World.* New York: Frederick Fell, 1968.

Martin, Dick. *The Executive's Guide to Handling a Press Interview.* New York: Pilot Books, 1977.

Maslow, Abraham H. *Toward a Psychology of Being.* New York: D. Van Nostrand Co., 1968.

Miller, Casey, and Kate Swift. *The Handbook of Nonsexist Writing.* New York: Barnes & Noble Books, 1980.

Monroe, Alan H. *Principles and Types of Speech.* New York: Scott, Foresman & Co., 1955.

Montgomery, Robert L. *Listening Made Easy.* New York: American Management Association, 1981.

Moore, Sam. *Negotiating Successfully.* New York: Time-Life Multimedia, 1975.

Morris, Desmond. *The Naked Ape.* New York: Dell Publishing Co., Inc. 1967.

———. *Manwatching: A Field Guide to Human Behavior.* New York: Harry N. Abrams Publishers, 1977.

Morris, Desmond, Peter Collet, Peter Marsh, and Marie O'Shaugnessy. *Gestures.* Briarcliff Manor, N.Y.: Stein & Day, 1979.

Morris, John O. *Make Yourself Clear!* New York: McGraw-Hill, 1972.

Morrisey, George L. *Effective Business & Technical Presentations.* Reading, Mass.: Addison-Wesley Publishing Co.-MOR Associates, 1982.

Moscovitch, Rosalie. *What's In A Word.* Boston: Houghton Mifflin Co., 1985.

Moustakas, Clark E. *Turning Points.* Englewood Cliffs, N.J.: Prentice-Hall, Inc., 1977.

Naisbitt, John. *Megatrends: Ten New Directions Transforming Our Lives.* New York: Warner Books, 1982.

Newman, Edwin. *Strictly Speaking.* New York: Warner Books, 1975.

———. *A Civil Tongue.* New York: Warner Books, 1977.

Nichols, William, ed. *The Best of Words to Live By.* New York: Essandess Special Editions, 1967.

Nierenberg, Gerald I. *The Art of Negotiating: Psychological Strategies for Gaining Advantageous Bargains.* New York: Cornerstone Library Publications, 1968.

———. *How to Give and Receive Advice.* New York: Pocket Books, 1975.

Nierenberg, Gerald I., and Henry H. Calero. *How to Read a Person Like a Book.* New York: Pocket Books, 1971.

———. *Meta-Talk.* New York: Pocket Books, 1974.

Nirenberg, Jesse S. *Getting Through to People.* Englewood Cliffs, N.J.: Prentice-Hall, Inc., 1963.

Novak, William, and Moshe Waldoks. *The Big Book of Jewish Humor.* New York: Harper & Row Publishers, 1981.

O'Brien, Richard. *Publicity: How to Get It.* New York: Barnes & Noble Books, 1978.

Parker, Dorothy. *The Viking Portable Library Dorothy Parker.* New York: Viking Press, 1944.

Paxson, William C. *The Business Writing Handbook.* New York: Bantam Books, Inc., 1981.

Payne, Stanley L. *The Art of Asking Questions.* Princeton, N.J.: Princeton University Press, 1951.

Peale, Norman Vincent. *The Power of Positive Thinking*. Englewood Cliffs, N.J.: Prentice-Hall, Inc., 1952.

Pendleton, Winston K. *Complete Speaker's Galaxy of Funny Stories, Jokes and Anecdotes*. West Nyack. N.Y.: Parker Publishing Co., Inc., 1981.

Peters, Thomas J., and Robert H. Waterman, Jr. *In Search of Excellence: Lessons from America's Best-Run Companies*. New York: Harper & Row Publishers, 1982.

Phillips, Leroy. *Peter Piper's Practical Principles of Plain and Perfect Pronunciation*. New York: Dover Publications, Inc., 1970.

Pickens, Jim. *The Closers*. Placerville, Calif.: Hampton House Publishing Co., 1980.

Piper, Watley. *The Little Engine That Could*. New York: Platt & Munk Publishers, 1954.

Postman, Neil. *Crazy Talk, Stupid Talk*. New York: Delta Books, 1976.

Pleninger, Andrew. *How to Survive and Market Yourself in Management*. New York: American Management Association, 1977.

Prochnow, Herbert V. *1,497 Jokes, Stories and Anecdotes: A Speaker's Handbook*. New York: Sterling Publishing Co., Inc., 1985.

Prochnow, Herbert V., and Herbert V. Prochnow, Jr. *The Public Speaker's Treasure Chest*. New York: Harper & Row Publishers, 1942.

Provost, Gary. *The Freelance Writer's Handbook*. New York: New American Library, 1982.

Qubein, Nido R., *Communicate Like a Pro*. Englewood Cliffs, N.J.: Prentice-Hall, Inc., 1983.

———. *Get the Best from Yourself: The Complete System of Personal and Professional Development*. Englewood Cliffs, N.J.: Prentice-Hall, Inc., 1983.

———. *Nido Qubein's Professional Selling Techniques*. Englewood Cliffs, N.J.: Prentice-Hall, Inc., 1983.

Ringer, Robert J. *Winning Through Intimidation*. Greenwich, Conn.: Fawcett, 1974.

Ritt, Thomas C., Jr. *Understanding Yourself, Then Others*. Ocean, N.J.: People Concepts, 1980.

Roget's International Thesaurus. 4th ed. New York: Harper & Row Publishers, 1977.

Saint-Exupery, Antoine de. *The Little Prince*. New York: Harcourt, Brace & World, 1943.

Safran, Louis A. *2000 Insults for All Occasions*. New York: Pocket Books, 1967.

Sarnoff, Dorothy. *Speech Can Change Your Life*. New York. Dell Publishing Co., Inc., 1972.

Schuller, Robert M. *You Can Become the Person You Want to Be*. New York: Pillar, 1976.

Schwartz, Roslyn. *The Smoker's Dictionary*. New York: Linden Press/Simon & Schuster, Inc., 1984.

Schwartz, Tony. *The Responsive Chord*. Garden City, N.Y.: Anchor Press/Doubleday, 1973.

Seuss, Dr. *Green Eggs and Ham*. New York: Random House, Inc., 1960.

Seyler Athene, and Stephen Haggard. *The Craft of Comedy*. New York: Theatre Art Books, 1966.

Shefter, Harry. *How to Prepare Talks and Oral Reports*. New York: Pocket Books, 1963.

Simon, Sidney B. *Negative Criticism and What You Can Do About It*. Allen, Tex.: Argus Communications, 1978.

Simpson, James B., comp. *Contemporary Quotations*. New York: Thomas Y. Crowell Co., 1964.

Skinner, Edith Warman. *Speak with Distinction*. New Brunswick, N.J.: N.p., 1965.

Slung, Michelle. *More Momilies*. New York: Ballantine Books, Inc., 1986.

Snell, Frank. *How to Hold a Better Meeting*. New York: Cornerstone Library, 1979.

———. *How to Stand Up and Speak Well in Business*. New York: Cornerstone Library, 1979.

Starr, Douglas P. *How to Handle Speechwriting Assignments*. New York: Pilot Books, 1978.

Strunk, William, Jr., and E. B. White. *The Elements of Style*. 2d ed. New York: Macmillan Publishing Co., Inc., 1972.

Tarrant, John J. *How to Negotiate a Raise*. New York: Pocket Books, 1976.

Toward Better Speech. New York: The Board of Education of the City of New York, 1953.

Trahey, Jane. *Jane Trahey on Women and Power*. New York: Avon Books, 1978.

Trillin, Calvin. *With All Disrespect*. New York: Penguin Books, 1986.

Turco, Lewis. *The Book of Forms: A Handbook of Poetics*. E. P. Dutton & Co., Inc., 1968.

Viorst, Judith. *It's Hard to Be Hip over Thirty and Other Tragedies of Married Life*. New York: New American Library, 1970.

Wallace, Amy, David Wallechinsky, and Irving Wallace. *The People's Almanac Presents The Book of Lists #2*. New York: Bantam Books, 1983.

Wallace, Amy, David Wallechinsky, Irving Wallace, and Sylvia Wallace. *The People's Almanac Presents The Book of Lists #3*. New York: Bantam Books, 1980.

Weinberg, George. *Self Creation*. New York: Avon Books, 1978.

Weintraub, Joseph. *The Wit and Wisdom of Mae West*. New York: Perigree Books/G.P. Putnam's Sons, 1967.

Weiss, Allen. *Write What You Mean: A Handbook of Business Communication*. New York: American Management Association, 1977.

Welsh, James J. *The Speech Writing Guide—Professional Techniques for Regular and Occasional Speakers*. New York: John Wiley & Sons, Inc., 1968.

White, E. B., and K. S. White, eds. *A Subtreasury of American Humor*. New York: Random House, Inc., 1941.

Wilde, Larry. *The Official Politician's Joke Book.* New York: Bantam Books, 1984.

Williams, Beryl. *Communicating Effectively.* Wellingborough, U.K.: Thomson Publishers Ltd., 1977.

Zinsser, William. *On Writing Well.* 2d. ed. New York: Harper & Row Publishers, 1980.

Postscript

Dorothy Leeds's presentations, both live and on tape, will help you manage better, communicate more effectively, and improve your image and relationships. More importantly, they will help you to take your knowledge and use it.

If you want to know more about Dorothy Leeds's speeches, seminars, and audiocassette programs, please call or write to:

> Dorothy Leeds, President
> Organizational Technologies, Inc., Suite 10A
> 800 West End Avenue
> New York, NY 10025
> (212) 864-2424

Her Positive Action Cassette Learning Programs are the following:

PowerSpeak: The Complete Guide to Persuasive Public Speaking and Presenting. You can easily become a powerful and persuasive presenter by following Dorothy Leeds's proven PowerSpeak method. Learn how to overcome the six major speaking faults. The set of six cassettes and the Comprehensive Workbook costs $95.

The Motivational Manager: How to Get Top Performance from Your Staff. Being an excellent manager is the best way to get ahead. With this motivational program you will discover your strengths and weaknesses, how to hire, coach, train, motivate, and lots more. The set of six cassettes and The Management Performance Indicator costs $95.

People Reading: Strategies for Engineering Better Relationships in Business. Gain a huge career advantage by influencing others and achieving results through reading the unique differences in people. The set of three cassettes and the Practical People Reading Guide costs $49.95.

How to Market Yourself and Get the Job of Your Choice. This is the system for people who want to be paid what they are worth. The set of two cassettes and Complete Workbook with Marketing Letter costs $39.95.

The System for Change. You can change and enrich your life, increase your opportunities, and help your staff to do the same. The cassette costs $14.95.

Super Sampling for Sales People: The Smart Questions System and The PowerSpeak System. Targeted condensations of two of Dorothy Leeds's highly acclaimed presentations. The cassette costs $18.95.

Save $53.80: Order all six programs for only $260.

Index

About the Author

Success is turning knowledge into positive action.
—D. Leeds

As one of America's most sought-after speakers, DOROTHY LEEDS has keynoted hundreds of conventions for organizations such as the National Speakers Association, Sales and Marketing Executives, The American Lung Association, Meeting Planners International, and The New York Society of Association Executives. She also frequently addresses corporate meetings for companies like Merrill Lynch and Digital Equipment. More than twenty thousand executives and salespeople, in such prestigious companies as Mobil Oil, Duke Power Company, and Prudential Bache, have been trained to be better communicators through Dorothy's unique programs of information and inspiration.

Dorothy Leeds is the author of the best seller *Smart Questions: A New Strategy for Successful Managers*, published by McGraw-Hill, which is now into its fifth printing and the featured selection of five major book clubs.

From the financial services industry to women's organizations to Fortune 500 companies, Dorothy has proved to be a popular favorite, asked to return again and again. Sharing her experience and success in her varied careers, from Broadway actress to knitwear manufacturer, to advertising executive, and now as president of Organizational Technologies, Inc., consultants in management, sales, and communications, Dorothy has addressed more than two thousand audiences, organized and conducted seminars and workshops, and set up corporate speaker's bureaus.

A well-known media personality, she has appeared on the "Tonight Show" and has been a frequent guest on radio and television programs across the United States.

Married and the mother of two children, Dorothy is a native New Yorker and lives in Manhattan. She is also a physical fitness enthusiast, who attributes her success to devoting positive energy to all areas of her life—a commitment that helped her overcome cancer and maintain a successful family and business life.

Books by
MICHAEL LeBOEUF, Ph. D.

DR. ROBERT ANTHONY

__**THE ULTIMATE SECRETS OF TOTAL SELF-CONFIDENCE** 0-425-10170-3/$3.95

Join the successful people who have mastered the principles of Total Self-Confidence. Put all aspects of your life under your control.

__**DR. ROBERT ANTHONY'S MAGIC POWER OF SUPER PERSUASION** 0-425-10981-X/$3.50

Simple, but powerful. Strengthen your art of communication and be a top achiever!

__**50 GREAT IDEAS THAT CAN CHANGE YOUR LIFE** 0-425-10421-4/$3.50

Fifty concepts designed to make self-evaluation easier than ever.

__**DR. ROBERT ANTHONY'S ADVANCED FORMULA FOR TOTAL SUCCESS**

0-425-10804-X/$3.95

Using simple step-by-step methods, turn your dreams into a reality of total success!

THE THINK BOOKS

In today's fast-paced, mixed-up world, Dr. Robert Anthony's THINK books offer solutions of hope, encouragement, and cheer. Every book contains 80 ideas, each on a separate perforated page—so you can easily tear out the ones you want to tack up or take with you!

__THINK 0-425-08747-6/$2.95

__THINK AGAIN 0-425-09572-X/$2.95

__THINK ON 0-425-11186-5/$2.95